Witness to Grace

Witness to Grace

A TESTIMONY OF FAVOR

W. FRANKLYN RICHARDSON

THE CHURCH ONLINE

Published by
The Church Online, LLC
1000 Ardmore Blvd.
Pittsburgh, PA 15221

Witness to Grace: A Testimony of Favor

ISBN: 978-1-940786-86-5

Library of Congress Number:

*Cover Photography and Cover Design by Suzanne Delawar Studio
Consultation by Michelle Necole Designs*

*This book is printed on acid free paper.
Printed in the USA*

For Inez, my gift of grace.

"…By the grace of God, I am what I am…"

I Corinthians 15:10

Acknowledgments

I OWE A GREAT DEBT TO SO MANY WHO HAVE TOUCHED MY life and made this work possible, many who now reside in the silent city where my parents live. Without them I would have no story. A special word of gratitude is reserved for my Project Assistant Velma McKenzie-Orr who gave herself totally to this effort. Her dedication, competence, encouragement, and focus were critical to the completion of this project. She was thorough and always available, late at night and early in the morning. She was my liaison between the publisher and me.

I am thankful for all of my team at Grace Church whose input was vital to the outcome of this work, especially my Assistant Anita Middleton, who navigated my schedule, making time available for this effort, and members of Grace Literary Arts Ministry (GLAM), who assisted in proofing this project.

I am grateful to my Project Manager Melissa K. Wharton and the other professionals at The Church Online whose zealous attention to every detail successfully navigated this project through the choppy waters of publication to completion.

I profoundly appreciate those who read sections of the manuscript and gave invaluable suggestions: Dr. Gregory Howard, Dr. Dwight C. Jones, Dr. Wallis C. Baxter III, Dr. Hakim J. Lucas, Dr. Riggins Earl, Reverend Al Sharpton, Dr. Boise Kimber, Dr. LaKeesha Walrond, Bishop John Bryant, Mr. Ted Jemison, Ms. Jacqueline L. Burton, Dr. Ralph Douglas West, Archbishop E. Bernard Jordan, and General Secretary and President Jim Winkler.

I am so thankful and proud of Howard John Wesley for his ministry and preaching, and for the time that he dedicated to write the Foreword for my memoir. He is indeed a son of whom I am well pleased.

Finally, to my wife Inez Golda Richardson for always being available for loving, honest critique and reflection on the details of my journey. To my son Pastor William F. Richardson III for his review of the manuscript and helpful advice. I am thankful as well for the renewing affectionate encouragement of my daughters, Katrina and Orchid.

While I am grateful for all the input I received, I take full responsibility for what is here presented. It is solely my work by the grace of God.

W. Franklyn Richardson

Scarsdale, New York 2020

Content

Foreword

I OFTEN STAND IN THE PULPIT OF THE ALFRED STREET Baptist Church in Alexandria, Virginia, where I serve as pastoral servant, look out over the amazing people that come to worship, listen to the melodious songs of praise, hear testimony of the many ways we seek to touch people with the transformative love of Jesus, become aware of the tremendous growth in Spirit and resources that God has given, and ask the question, "Lord, how did I get here?" How did God choose and then place me in such a wonderful situation of which I know I am not worthy? That is a question we all are humbled to ask at some point in our life's journey: how could someone so unworthy be the recipient of something so amazing? W. Franklyn Richardson knows the answer that is universally valid for each and every one of us—*grace*.

To me, W. Franklyn Richardson is more than a pastor, more than a civic and community leader, more than a denominational and religious icon, more than a scholar, more than a preacher. He is part of God's grace that has been operating in my life for more than 30 years. When I was called to preach at the age of seventeen under the pastoral leadership of my father, the late Rev. Dr. Alvin J. Wesley, his small church in Chicago was the only model of ministry I had ever seen. I was blessed to have a father who saw and dreamed of more for me than I did for myself. He believed, long before I did, that God had something special in store and planned for me as a fourth-generation Baptist preacher, and he wanted me to see what God was able to do.

He reached out to his friend, W. Franklyn Richardson, and asked a tremendous favor. My senior year in high school required a month-long internship in our anticipated career field, and my father asked Dr. Richardson if I could come to Mt. Vernon for a month and shadow him at Grace Baptist Church to see what excellence in ministry was and what grace could do.

As a child of the National Baptist Convention, I was awed and intimidated by his presence. He was the general secretary of the largest Black Baptist religious body in the world and I had watched him from a distance, never thinking or dreaming that I would meet him personally. Imagine my amazement when he said, "Yes" to my father's request. He flew me to Mt. Vernon, moved me into his home with his family, took me everywhere with him for a month, and provided me with an intimate exposure to his life and his ministry. When you realize that you have been the recipient of grace, you have no hesitation in being a conduit of grace for others. My first vision of grace at work in ministry and pastoral life was provided by W. Franklyn Richardson, and from that time in 1990 until today he has been my model and my mentor. When my father died in 2006, I began calling Dr. Richardson "Dad," and when I see what God has done in my own life and how God has used me in ministry and wonder how, "Dad" is part of that answer.

Witness to Grace is the world's opportunity to get a glimpse and insight into the life that has blessed me and has been a conduit of grace to countless others. Hear the eye-witness testimony of a life that has paused in meditative reflection and has come to the conclusion that grace is sufficient. Listen to the humble beginnings of inherited generational slavery and racism. Hear the stories of disappointment and perceived failure. See the personal struggle and even anger with God. Share in the wonder of the plans God had and has revealed in this life. And ultimately be amazed at all the various dimensions of grace and how God operates.

In 1994, I witnessed Dr. Richardson's heart break as he lost the election and bid to become president of the National Baptist Convention. I heard the rumoring and prophetic predictions of his demise and the inescapable stain of failure. Yet here he stands more than 25 years later, with an unequalled tenure of service to the universal and ecumenical body of Christ, unparalleled leadership in national economic initiatives, recognized scholarship and homiletical integrity as one of the greatest preachers of our time, and more than four decades of pastoral leadership at the providentially and appropriately named, Grace Baptist Church in Mt. Vernon, New York. His life is a witness to grace.

But *Witness to Grace* is much more than one man's story. This is not simply another autobiography. This is not some self-aggrandizing testimony. This is much more than a walk down memory lane. This is a theological and inspirational life lesson about God's presence and God's promises and God's provisions for all who read it.

I recently took my sons to see a movie that was offered in 3D. We were given our glasses and sat down to watch the movie. When the movie began, I noticed that my youngest son did not have his glasses on. I encouraged him to put them on. When he asked why, I responded "Because there's so much you'll miss without them." Likewise, in *Witness to Grace*, Dr. Richardson encourages us to put on our glasses and view our own lives through the prism of grace and see the amazing things grace has done and is doing for us. He broadens our understanding of grace and reveals grace at work in unexpected people and painful places of our lives.

He shows us the generational grace that was at work in our lives before we breathed our first breath. He destroys the narrow constraints of grace that too many of us have employed that have caused us to miss how wonderful God truly is. And most importantly, he teaches us how to take true inventory of grace at work in our lives to recognize that no matter what your station or situation of life, you are the product of grace and therefore have a reason to hope and a foundation for faith. Journey into these pages that bear *Witness to Grace* and allow W. Franklyn Richardson to be for you what he is for me: a conduit of God's grace in your own life.

Dr. Howard John Wesley

Prologue

I DECLARE, HERE AND NOW, THAT I AM A WITNESS TO GRACE! When someone declares they are a Witness to Grace, they are declaring they have had a firsthand encounter with God. There are times when I am overwhelmed by the notion of grace—times when feelings of immense gratitude flood my soul. I have longed to place these thoughts on paper. The swift movement of time, the burden of responsibility, and the hesitancy to revisit the pain of some of my experiences have delayed the initiation and completion of this work. However, I must say that the writing process has mellowed the pain and deepened my understanding of how God's purpose can function in our disappointment. His thoughts are not our thoughts, and His ways are not our ways (Isaiah 55:8), but His love is ever constant.

Viewing life through the prism of the grace of God is optional and is an option that has blessed me. We don't have to view life through the window of grace. We can choose to see our blessings as a manifestation of our efforts—a viewpoint that may ultimately lead to hopelessness and despair.

When we truly acknowledge the presence and function of grace in our lives, we never feel cheated. On the contrary, we know that we have experienced God's provision completely undeserved, and this opens the door for us to express authentic gratitude, which results in a positive attitude and an optimistic expectation. It causes new blessings to emerge with pregnant potential on the dawning of each morning. I feel undeserving, which I believe is the foundation of authentic gratitude.

I am not writing my experience in this manner because it is unique. Rather, I write these words as my contribution to the great chorus of all who testify to the amazing grace of God. It is my testimony. It is an acknowledgment of God's fingerprints on my journey—a journey rich and wonderful. I have come to know God's favor, and I am grateful for it. Within the pages of this book, I do not speak of grace within the narrow view of salvation from sin exclusively but in the belief that all of life, what was, and is, and is to come, testifies to His grace!

As we move forward in faith, discovering grace is a retrospective, meditative experience. We look back over our shoulders to discover what God has done. We come to see the grace of God as we examine the journey which we have undertaken. The foundational attitude for discovering grace is a sense of unworthiness, the idea that we have received more than we have earned. This notion awakens a grace consciousness in each of us, and this is what I hope to pass on to you as you read these pages.

Grace is God being available and accessible. Grace is the character, essence, and unmerited divine favor of God. The entire cosmic collaboration, from the sloping valleys to the majestic stars, to the roaring seas, to the crawling lizard, to the galloping stallions in the field, to the budding flowers, to the singing birds, and to all humankind, is the result of the function of grace.

Years ago, I heard the Reverend Manuel Scott Sr. of the St. John Baptist Church in Dallas, TX, preach about multiple expressions of God's grace as observed in the Genesis narrative of creation. He described them as Geological Grace (the grace of land and sea), Anthropological Grace (the grace of persons), Agricultural Grace (the grace of provision), and Astronomical Grace (the grace of the stars, the sun, and the moon). Each form of grace, he suggests, we did not purchase, but God gave it to us freely.

I acknowledge all of these unique physical expressions of God's grace. I must add to it what I consider to be the most marvelous expression of His grace: His presence. God's abiding companionship, both in the presence of His Son Jesus Christ and the Holy Spirit, is the ultimate gift of grace. I have known the gift of His presence and benefited from His thoughts towards me.

I have not come to this moment with any sense of self-righteousness. I admit that my brokenness has often been the result of my actions, and I have been the recipient of an abundance of grace and mercy. I see mercy as an aspect of God's grace. Mercy is the pain that God chooses to withhold from me that I deserve, and grace is the favor which God decides to bless me with that I don't deserve. To be sure, I am grateful for his mercy.

This book is about His grace in all its dimensions. It is about God's aggressive participation in favoring the life of an undeserving believer. This book is about how the impact of His grace, which may often be a corrective rearranging of events that suggest failure. What I demonstrate in this book are the incidences of God's grace as a corrective presence in my life. He has turned failure into triumph and obstruction into opportunity. This corrective presence is at the heart of my Christology.

This book is the presentation of my understanding of a loving God who gave up His perfect best to save a wretched worst: "He paid an awful debt He did not owe, a debt we owed and could not pay." Oh, grace, that saved a wretch like me. May these shared reflections of grace, discovered and affirmed, prompt a fresh awakening in you of the thread of grace woven in the fabric of your life.

Witness to Grace

CHAPTER ONE

Mad at God

It was September 1994. I was standing alone in the convention hall at the Super Dome in New Orleans with tears running down my cheeks. I was disappointed, despaired, and disillusioned. I was mad as hell at God! But I did not know it at that moment. I suppressed the truth of what I truly felt about what God had permitted. My anger for the moment obscured all that God had been to me and done for me.

I was standing there defeated, pondering the outcome of the presidential election of the National Baptist Convention, USA, Inc. I had served for thirteen years as general secretary. In September 1982, Dr. T. J. Jemison was elected president of the convention. Based on his recommendation, I was elected general secretary at age thirty-two and followed Dr. Jemison's twenty-nine-year tenure in that office. When his tenure as president ended. I ran to succeed him and lost.

Being angry with God and questioning Him at that moment may be the highest form of faith. To be angry with God is not disrespect, nor is query blasphemy. It is the last resort of a believer's frustration: addressing the only one who has the answer. He may not answer or may simply say, "Get over it." This time, the process of divine query brought me to a place of fresh discovery.

The suppression of one's disappointment with God is advanced by the guilt of being angry with God. Being confused by God's actions leaves you in a dark place. It took much prayer and reflection for me to own and engage with the anger I felt. It required me to be confessional, especially against the backdrop of my grandmother's early admonition to never question God.

Emma Richardson Williams was my paternal grandmother and she was born in Irmo, South Carolina. Her grandmother was enslaved. My grandmother, like most of her contemporaries from the South, had an unwavering faith in God and was surrendered to His authority. Even in the face of the cruel inhumanity of slavery and racism, their faith left no room for questioning God.

When I was a lad, she would authoritatively declare; "You never ask God, 'Why?'" In her thinking, to question God was a form of distrust and ingratitude. I think it may have also been a way to survive the cruel hardship of her situation. To be sure, the faith of my forebears was authentic.

After experiencing the sting of failure, I was forced to focus on the broader presence of God in my life—not a narrow focus on a single event. All of us have known disappointment and despair at one time or another, but the gift of grace is to discover, in our disappointment and failure, lessons that prepare us to manage future opportunities for prosperity. The positive collateral consequence of failure may very well be that it sets us up to see the grace of God!

Days later I was rising out of my despair, secluded and sitting on the seashore listening to the waves and watching the glistening sun kiss the turquoise waters of the Caribbean. It came to me that I was so fortunate to be a beneficiary of the grace of God. All around me was evidence of His favor. I just needed to change my focus, open my mind and behold His goodness. The very embrace of the sun and sea was symbolic and literal evidence of the grace of God, not purchased or earned by me, but was, like it is to every other human, a cosmic gift of God. I recalled in that moment that there were multiple expressions of God's amazing grace in my life.

I found myself taking inventory of His goodness and mercy, a reflection that began with me pondering my origin and the fact that my forebears were slaves who survived the constraints of a denied humanity and overwhelming cruelty in juxtaposition to the opportunities and exposures I had been given. I am overwhelmed by God's love, patience, provision, and grace towards me and how what others have intended for evil, God intended for good. My life is empowered by the thought that not only did God intend positive purpose for our lives, but even in the face of determined adversaries committed to our detriment, He has the power to actualize His purpose on our behalf.

My ancestors were descendants of enslaved African Americans. My father, William Franklyn Richardson Sr., was born and raised in the racist South. He and his family were a part of the exploited Blacks who survived on the post-slavery plantations as sharecroppers. They grew, picked, and sold cotton to the plantation owner who made sure that their pay was equal to or less than what it cost them to raise the crop and survive. This arrangement guaranteed that they would always remain in debt.

My father went to school in a one-room shack with very limited resources and almost no books. My father did not meet his father, Frederick Bowers III, until he was a teenager and grew up nurtured by his mother, Emma, and his extended family in the close-knit community of Black sharecroppers. His father left South Carolina as part of the great migration from the South, never marrying his mother, and settled in Philadelphia in search of opportunity.

At fifteen years old, my father was accused of a "misspoke" by a White woman, which enraged the White community. Black people in the South, post reconstruction, were viewed as having no rights, a fact reinforced by local laws and the United States Constitution. Black men in particular were beaten and lynched for the smallest perceived infraction of the White superiority conduct code. Having been so accused, he had to leave South Carolina under the cover of night to avoid being severely beaten or worse by vigilantes pursuing him. He escaped to Baltimore, Maryland and in that moment, this fifteen-year-old Black boy was now in a strange city with no money, homeless, and with no way to support himself. By what seemed to be pure coincidence, he met a friend of his father who was able to send a letter to share the boy's circumstance. My grandfather replied swiftly with a letter of his own, instructing, "Send the boy to me." My father then left Baltimore, making the journey to Philadelphia where his father had migrated 15 years earlier. It was there in Philadelphia in 1940 that my father finally met his father for the first time.

When I consider what could have been the consequences for a vulnerable Black teenage boy sought after by enraged racist White men from the South, I am gratefully astonished by the grace of God functioning on my behalf and impacting my preexistence for good. It is clear to me that God intentioned me. I am no coincidence but am the byproduct of divine intentionality. If my father's situation had ended differently, I, but for the grace of God, might never have been born.

After sharing this story with my twelve-year-old granddaughter Addison, she replied, "And me too, Papa!" She is, in fact, further evidence of prearranged grace, as are my children and all of our grandchildren. Each one of us is the result of divine intention. Our mere existence is evidence of God's intention to favor us with life. Every breath we take, every step we make is grace! Essentially, we all have our origins in the grace of God. We, each of us, are a gift of God. Not one person comes into the world without a divine passport. God's grace is deposited in all of our DNA.

At the University of Pennsylvania hospital early Tuesday morning, June 14, 1949, I was presented and given access to this glorious creation provided by the omnipotence of a loving God. Grace was compounded by the escort of two devoted parents, William Franklyn Richardson Sr. and Amanda Florine Ellison Richardson, who nurtured me with unconditional love while developing in me an awakened spirituality. In my home, the existence of God was never a question. It was a presumption validated by faith. My brother Ronald, my sister Vickilyn, and I never knew a time where God was not acknowledged as a reliable component of our existence.

My early years were marked by the cocooning embrace of my parents, seen in their care and concern for us, expressed in words and deeds. I felt exceptionally close to my mother in those early years. She was warm and happy, and I delighted being in her presence. I came to know her as a woman of authentic faith, which she exercised in the daily struggles of her life. I saw how she trusted God completely.

When I was a teenager, she gave me a front row seat to how she dealt in faith with the challenges of her life. I did not know at the time that she was in fact modeling behavior for how I would come to live my own life in faith. I recall coming home from school one day and saw her sitting at the kitchen table with tears streaming down her face. The monthly bills were laid out before her. I had never seen my mother so distraught. I asked her, "Momma, what's wrong?"

She replied to me without looking at me, "I am trying to make ends meet." Then she turned to me and smiled, "The Lord will make a way." She relied on the ultimate grace of God in every aspect of her life.

My mother cultivated the soil upon which she would deposit seeds of faith in each of her children's lives. After the passing of many years, I still recall the intimate conversations I had with my mother about faith in God. She was so hospitable to my elementary query about how one comes to know God in their life. She gave me space to ask the most fundamental questions without embarrassment. She encouraged my personal pursuit to know God for myself. No question was too simple for her serious consideration.

I remember one day, not long after I accepted Christ and joined the church, my mother and I were riding in the car. In my fresh enthusiasm and excitement, I said, "Mom I have such strong faith in God, I believe I could cut my arm off and my faith would put it back on."

She responded very cautiously, like an acrobat on a tight rope, making sure that her response did not cause me to lose my beginning spiritual balance. "You do not have to hurt yourself to prove your faith. Life will bring you opportunities to exercise your faith. Whatever may come in your life, God will see you through." My mother was my tutor in faith. Her early advice still informs my relationship with God.

My father, like my mother, had a strong faith in God. He did not articulate it the way she did, but he always expressed a profound acknowledgement of the grace of God operating in his life.

My father was a reliable presence in my life, firm as a rock. He was the authority figure in our home. He was the final word—the Supreme Court. He wanted to teach us responsibility and accountability. He wanted me to be a man's man. Looking back, I think his expectations for me were somewhat influenced by his growing up without a father in his life. He was motivational in his relationship with me. He always wanted me to achieve, whether on the baseball diamond or the football field or in the classroom. He wanted very much for me to succeed in life. His favorite advice for his children was "Whatever you do, be the best. If you are a garbage man, be the best garbage man you can be."

One day I rushed in the house from elementary school, huffing and puffing. To my surprise, my father was home. He saw my disarray and with a furrowed brow asked, "What's wrong?"

"There is a boy chasing me," I said, breathing hard. "He threatens to beat me up every day after school." The boy, Abraham, was a rough fellow. He bullied all the kids in the neighborhood and had a reputation for being a good fighter. Most of us were afraid of him. But my dad told me that day to go back outside and find Abraham.

He looked at me stone-faced and said, "You beat him or I beat you." Given that mandate, I rose above my fears and followed my father's instructions to the letter. Mission accomplished. I returned home to my father's warm embrace and further counsel to not allow fear of anyone or anything to diminish my self-confidence, and that lesson still empowers me to this day.

I remember coming home from my first semester in college after being licensed as an intern in ministry. My father, who had to make extreme sacrifices to pay my first semester's tuition, joyfully announced that he had just hit the number (a form of local, illegal lottery) and that he was thankful that he could meet my second semester tuition obligation.

"Gambling? That's the devil's money," I said with naiveté and self-indulgent righteousness.

My father rolled his eyes and replied, "Sure, the devil might have brought it, but the Lord sure sent it." I felt those words. They arrested me and challenged the constraints that I had placed on God's grace.

God's grace not only shows up in sanctioned places of faith but in rejected places and rejected people. It is the fundamental character of grace to embrace the unmerited and the undeserving. My father's ability to see the grace of God beyond the boundaries of one's immediate context was and continues to be instructive to me. I cannot count the times that God has shown up in the unexpected for me.

My immediate family included two loving siblings. My brother, Ronald, was next to me in age and my sister, Vickilyn, was the youngest. Both were exceptionally gifted musically and excelled in their careers. Ronald was a critically acclaimed Tony-award-winning Broadway actor. Vickilyn is an actor who has performed on stage and screen. My parents provided the best they could for us as children. They worked hard every day, even if there were days when it was hard to meet the needs of our family. We were not categorized as poor. We were a working-class family, but we had some poor days. My parents seldom had excess, but we always had sufficiency and an overabundance of love. In addition, they gave huge doses of inspiration and encouragement. We were their priority.

I grew up with clearly defined boundaries without feeling confined. I saw my parents exercise extraordinary confidence in God as we passed through difficult days. God never abandoned us. His grace was visible every step of the way. At Christmas, Mom and Dad were very pensive about how they were going to provide the tangible aspects of Christmas for their children. They no doubt felt the pressures of the

American consumer culture and its advocacy of materialistic values surrounding the season. We had the nontangible aspects of Christmas. The spirit of Christmas came alive by our faith and awakened spirituality. Amazingly, my parents always found a way to make each Christmas one to remember. From nuts and fruits on the tables to gifts under the tree, all of it demonstrated to me visible signs of God's amazing grace. I grew up shrouded under the influence of faith that was presented in every aspect of my life as a child.

Early on, my father's mother came to live with us with my mother's enthusiastic endorsement. She became my personal escort into the life of the church: Sunday school, youth choir, prayer meetings, vacation Bible school, Easter pageants and other activities. I accepted Christ as my savior at age seven and was baptized into the church on Easter Sunday, April 6, 1958. Thanks to these early encounters to engage my spirituality, the seeds that were planted in me blossomed into the full-blown faith that has carried me across the years. Oh, what favor to have known Him so early.

My mother's father, the Reverend Wade Clifton Ellison, a pastor of the Colored Methodist Episcopal (CME) in South Jersey, modeled the notion of ministry as a vocation for me. He had two brothers who were pastors, the Reverends Ernest Ellison and Joseph Ellison. My grandfather lived in close proximity to me. Grand Pop had an affinity for gardening, coupled with an entrepreneurial ambition that caused him to show up in Philadelphia on Saturday mornings, with fresh vegetables and fruit from his gardens in New Jersey, to sell his wares from his truck. At ten years old, I could not wait for his arrival so that I could help sell what he had brought and holler through the neighborhood, "Tomatoes, potatoes, watermelon!" A strong bond grew between this bi-vocational minister and his grandson. There were many ways that this relationship provided a precursor to my early-engaged thinking about ministry. Growing up in his space, I had an intimate exposure to a pastor.

Every summer from my childhood years to my early teens, our parents would send us on the train escorted by our grandmother to spend a month with our father's family in the south to the ancestral home of my father in Irmo, South Carolina. My father would always drive down to pick us up. It was a visit that served at least three purposes: to give us a vacation, to get us out of the summer urban setting, and to give us an opportunity to get acquainted with our roots and extended members of our family. As I look back, these summer experiences expanded my exposure to my Southern origins.

I recall several impacting experiences as a result of my visits to South Carolina. These visits took place in the late 1950s through the mid-1960s. It was a time of unsettling racial tension and emerging civil rights protests in the South, bracketed by *Brown v. the Board of Education*, sit-ins," and the March on Washington. It was during these visits that I became acquainted with racism. Black people's resentment of racism was fermenting to an all-time high. I would come of age in this era—having grown up in the north and very young.

My trips to the South gave me a firsthand glimpse of discrimination and racial hostility at an early age. I remember boarding the train with my grandmother and my brother at Philadelphia's 30th Street Station with a shoebox containing fried chicken wrapped in wax paper. Years later I came to realize the greater significance of the shoebox lunch. Negroes, our racial identity during that time, could not buy lunch or eat in the dining car on the train. I further recall that when the train got to the Mason-Dixon Line, all Negroes had to move to the all-Black passenger cars at the rear of the train. I really did not understand what was happening as a child. I suppose, in an effort to protect me, no one explained the reason for the move. But as time went on, I came to understand and resent the train ride.

Once in South Carolina, we were guests of my father's brother Westly and his wife Roxy. They had four daughters, our first cousins, whom we enjoyed visiting. I recall their house being a pleasant Southern home with chickens in the yard. There was one encounter that stands out in my memory. We had been in Irmo, a little rural village, for about three weeks. We would frequent the local general store, which was within walking distance to their house, to buy candy, snacks, and sodas. On one occasion, my cousin returned from the store distraught and crying. When my uncle inquired what was wrong, my cousin said that the owner of the store asked her, "Have those niggers from the north gone back home yet?" She abruptly left the store and returned home. My uncle went to the store, addressed the owner and expressed his outrage. When he returned, he forbade all of us from going to that store ever again.

These early encounters with racism were revealing to me as a child and informed my future. Upon reflection, the response of my elders was instructive. First, the practice of using a shoebox response by Blacks to a racial indignity was creative, innovative, and pointed to the Black person's capacity to rise above systemic racism. As a child, I wondered where this hostility came from. What is it about me that triggered that hostile response in the general store owner? As time passed, I came to understand that those mild indignities pointed to more harsh and cruel actions of racism in American society, then and now. Yet when one considers the evil inflicted on Black people in this country, we not only continue to exist, we thrive. This is indicative that the grace of God still functions.

Moreover, those summer weeks with my family connected me to my legacy of faith and my cultural heritage. Irmo was the place where my enslaved forebears were settled after being brought through the Port of Charleston to an oppressive existence that was sustained for two and a half centuries. The next generations were freed to live as sharecroppers. They lived as custodians of hope with faith in God as their constant companion. Yet, another generation of empowered women and men rose above legal restraint to live in legal legitimacy, to become purveyors of legal judgment and drafters of legal legislation and occupiers of the highest legal authority. Oh, for grace what a privilege.

I speak of these events, persons, and experiences to express my view of what has laid the foundation for my encounter with life through the window of grace. What a marvelous platform God provided for the unfolding of my journey. It is a "testimony of favor."

CHAPTER TWO

The Fork in the Road

IN MY MORE FORMATIVE YEARS, I BEGAN TO REFLECT ON MY future, engaging the notion of faith at a more mature level. What had been a gentle tug to consider ministry as my life's work began to become more pronounced.

As a child, I was obsessed with the fascination of being a preacher to the extent that I would gather my sister, brother, cousins, and other children around the stoop of the entrance to our home and play church. I was always the preacher. As I became a teenager, the idea of being a preacher was less enticing, and I discouraged any suggestion of the sort. Ministry wasn't "cool" to me, but I remained very active in the life of the church through youth ministry, teenage choir, and junior ushers.

I was an industrious youth. My first job, where I had to be every workday, was sweeping up hair at Mr. Martinelli's barbershop down on the corner from my home. Next I shined shoes at Mr. Taylor's shoeshine stand around the corner from where we lived. I enjoyed work, something I hadn't considered ministry to be.

I enjoyed earning my own money, and in the eleventh grade I secured a job that would become the most memorable of my young adulthood. It was a full-time summer job assisting in the laboratory of the West Park Hospital. I worked with everything from blood protoplasm to tissue samples to autopsies. It was fascinating and opened my eyes to the vulnerabilities of human life and aspects of healthcare that I had never considered.

Having sufficiently suppressed the impulse to go into ministry, or so I thought, and prompted by new exposure to medicine and health care, I decided that I was going to explore the possibility of becoming a doctor. I was encouraged in my consideration by the hospital staff and particularly by Dr. Fink, chief of pathology, under whose supervision I worked in the lab, and Dr. Weinstein who was a general practitioner and chairman of the board of the hospital. The doctors promised that when I graduated from college, they would pay for my medical school. I was excited and challenged by their offer, and that settled my decision: I was going to be a doctor.

I returned to school for my final year and resumed my after-school job in the laboratory. My work at the hospital encouraged my decision to attend college and avail myself of the opportunity to take advantage of the generous offer that would allow me to become a doctor. However, when I went to discuss my plans with my high school counselor,

Mr. Dribin, he told me solemnly, "You are not college material." He suggested that I should consider a vocation instead of college. Needless to say, I left his office shattered and deeply discouraged, but I was determined to prove his assessment inaccurate.

My plans took a turn in November 1965 while I was walking home from school, I experienced a very sharp pain in my right side that proved to be appendicitis. My parents took me to the hospital, where the doctors recommended immediate surgery to remove my appendix. They did not give me general anesthesia but gave me a spinal procedure. Back then the spinal block was not widely used. Consequently, while the surgery was a success, there were complications. The effects of the spinal block did not wear off, as they should have, leaving me paralyzed longer than expected. The doctors were concerned. My parents and I were afraid, wondering when or if it would wear off.

During the three days that I was paralyzed, I reached out to God in prayer, acknowledging that I knew He called me to ministry. I promised that if He returned the feeling and mobility to my legs, I would preach the gospel—a promise I reneged on once I was well and out of the hospital.

The following June I graduated from high school and was admitted to West Philadelphia Community College (WPCC). I enrolled and matriculated in September, determined to proceed with my plan. I struggled that semester and ended up dropping out of WPCC. I couldn't get the voice of my high school counselor out of my head and began to believe that his conclusion that I was not college material was accurate.

After dropping out of WPCC, I began working at the funeral home for "Uncle Hank." Pennsylvania State Senator Freeman Hankins owned the funeral home and was a family friend and like an uncle to me. Uncle Hank was inspiring to me. Having access to a Black man who had achieved so much was encouraging to a young floundering teenager. One of my many chores at the funeral home was to assist in directing funeral services. One night, I walked into a service at a Pentecostal church where I was assigned to assist. I observed three young preachers conducting the service. Their faithfulness in their ministry reminded me of the unfulfilled promise that I made to God the year before. I was ashamed. I was a betrayer. I was deeply convicted. I went home and prayed, asking God to forgive me for breaking my promise. I surrendered to His will that night and have had inner peace in my life ever since. The God of another chance is a gift of grace.

I called my pastor, Reverend James Edward Hamlin, that night and confessed my call to ministry and asked for his prayers to go forward. He said to me, among other things, "I always knew that you would preach." He was encouraging and reassuring. Subsequent to our conversation about the meaning of my call and preparation for ministry, he scheduled a time for me to preach my initial sermon.

On Sunday May 28, 1967, I stepped into the pulpit of the Community Baptist Church at 40th and Spring Garden Street in Philadelphia before a host of family, friends and well-wishers. The subject of my sermon was "No Need to Want." My text was from Psalm 23:1, "The Lord is my shepherd; I shall not want."

The sermon at that time in my development was actually more a statement of hope fueled by an enthusiastic budding faith than a testimony of what I would later come to know to be true. I introduced the sermon with a very elementary understanding of the Bible, but the prevailing idea was that God would supply our need. Looking back, I probably needed to hear that more than anyone else in the church that night. Having been preaching now more than fifty years, the truth of that message is no longer speculation. I know for sure the Lord can supply our needs.

I felt a sense of fulfillment and purpose that night upon completing the sermon. After every sermon I have preached since that night, I have felt grace afresh, awed by the realization that He would use a wretch like me. What an overwhelming notion and profound act of grace!

In further discussion with Pastor Hamlin, I indicated that I wanted to be a prepared preacher, but I had performance challenges at West Philadelphia Community College that resulted in me having to drop out. After some reflection, Pastor Hamlin encouraged me to apply to Virginia Union University (VUU) because they had a stellar record in preparing Black preachers for ministry. That would become among the greatest advice that I would ever receive in my entire life.

Pathway to Hope

AFTER MUCH PRAYER AND REFLECTION, I MUSTERED THE courage to follow through on my pastor's advice and applied to Virginia Union University. My application was reviewed, and they requested a written essay from me, explaining why I wanted to study at VUU. Because of my GPA and poor transcripts, I had to take a test when I applied. After the VUU staff reviewed my test score, they learned that I had a reading deficiency that would require remediation. I was told that I would be given a conditional matriculation, subject to my performance during the first year. Only a Historically Black College or University (HBCU) would flex its criteria to make a way for a marginal Black student, not as an exception but as a normal course of procedure in fulfilling its mission.

I was a casualty of the inner-city schools of West Philadelphia that had just passed me along without ensuring that I had acquired the skills consistent with my graduation. I was essentially "not college material" because 1 had not been prepared for college. I could not read well and therefore could not perform. I never understood why it was so difficult to perform academically. Even my initial sermon's successful outcome was a surprise to me. I did not really understand why I failed at the community college. I did not know that I had a problem. Virginia Union University was the first to identify my reading impairment. I don't recall at what level 1 was reading, but 1 was significantly deficient. Without intervention, I am certain I would have stumbled through life.

Coming to Virginia Union was eye-opening and confidence-building in several ways for me. Prior to attending Virginia Union, I had never had a Black teacher or administrator. I had never been exposed to what might have been referred to as the "Black Elite." I had never seen a Black physician, nor had I experienced an organization where the ultimate controlling authority was in Black hands. Virginia Union was reassuring to me. It modeled before my eyes what I could become. I was empowered by what I saw. It is clear that one of the benefits of a Black college experience is that it builds confidence in Black students who grow up and live in a hostile, racist, self-esteem assaulting culture. Black schools are where Black youth can go to repair their self-esteem and realize that they are just as valuable as any other student and can reach just as high.

My first year at Virginia Union was filled with excitement. I approached it with enthusiasm as I experienced a fresh frontier as a student and beginning minister. College life was completely new to me, and I was completely satisfied with my life. Even then, I had a strong sense of the divine favor functioning in my life.

During the first year of my matriculation, having preached my initial sermon in Philadelphia and receiving a license by that congregation to practice preaching, I found great opportunity to preach in the rural communities of Virginia. There were mostly small congregations scattered throughout the adjoining counties to Richmond. Though a novice, my preaching found hospitality among the churches. Many of the churches did not have pastors and others needed preachers for revivals and special occasions. Invitations came from word of mouth or ministers would recommend me. It was a great way to gain experience and was a way for me, as a student, to earn much-needed income. I truly enjoyed that time in my life. The church was central to those communities and their worship was authentic, not highly sophisticated but highly spiritual.

As time went on, I got better. The churches were like a laboratory in worship. I learned early that to be a good preacher one must preach. The many opportunities to preach sharpened my skills in ways no classroom could.

I completed my first year at VUU and went on to find a pathway to academic achievement under the affirming care of a dedicated faculty and staff. My professors were competent and committed. They functioned to expose me to the world of the mind. Among them were Dr. Marcelious Toney who taught biology, Dr. Pearl Mankins who taught history, Dr. John Malcus, the 4th President of the University who taught sociology, and Dr. Rafael Hernandez who taught Spanish. Virginia Union salvaged me!

I shudder to think what would have been the outcome of my life had it not been for the historical Black college, not only for me but the thousands of young men and women who would have been on the human junk pile of wasted potential had it not been for HBCUs. What a loss it would have been for those students, this nation, and the world. We never would have known the bright light of promise buried in the DNA of a devalued humanity. Legions of classrooms would never have seen the illuminating promise of nurturing teachers and professors. The sick would be deprived of competent, compassionate, and committed nurses and physicians, court rooms would be devoid of the compelling arguments for justice put forward by brilliant legalists, and the gallant oratory filling the sanctuaries of churches across the length and breadth of America and the majestic swells of musical magic that would fill concert halls and cathedrals would be silent without HBCUs. There would be no Martin Luther King Jr., Oprah Winfrey, Lawrence Douglas Wilder, Charles Drew, Earl Gilbert Graves Jr., Gardner Calvin Taylor, Thurgood Marshall, Jessye Norman, or Samuel Lee Gravely, Jr., just to name a few.

I have no doubt that HBCUs are salvaging stations for millions, denied their humanity and opportunity, where they can find capacity and validation. Virginia Union was such a place for me. It was a place where opportunity and preparation intersected. I am more than certain that the lifeboats of possibility that HBCUs represented in the past are still vital today to the success of hundreds of thousands of minorities trapped in pockets of disadvantage across the landscape of this nation.

In the opening days of my college experience, I found affirmation when my peers elected me president of the freshman class. It was a platform for an emerging self-confidence that would manifest in leadership opportunities to come. It was an affirmation that arrested my anxiety. I was subsequently elected president of the sophomore class and vice president of the Student Government Association.

I entered college in September 1967 during the Vietnam War era. Many of my friends were being drafted. As a matter of fact, one of my friends from my home church, Alvin Watkins, was killed in combat in Vietnam the summer before I began matriculation. I anticipated that I would be drafted, and I was prepared to go even though I was against the war, influenced by the positions of Dr. Martin Luther King Jr. and the anti-war movement. After entering Virginia Union as a freshman with the intention of preparing for ministry, I discovered during discussions with my classmates that a student pursuing ministry was eligible for military deferment. Upon receiving that information, I went to the office of the dean for the school of religion to inquire about how I might qualify. I met with the dean, Dr. Allix Bledsoe James, who would later become my mentor and would ultimately become president of the university.

I recall walking into his office acting overly accomplished. After an exchange of greetings, I introduced myself as the Reverend Richardson and that I had come to inquire about military deferment for ministerial students to which he began to deflate my heightened ego. He replied, "Who said you were a minister? You have just begun college." I tried to explain that my home church and pastor had licensed me to preach. When I left his office, I recognized that I had just begun and did not know whether he would apply for my deferment. It was indeed a healthy deflation of an exaggerated ego. He ultimately applied for my exemption and it was granted.

As I reflect on the occurrences that placed me on the road to fulfilling my purpose, it is as though God's hand reached down from glory to navigate my preparation to be His servant.

During the second semester of my freshman year, members of the service fraternity Alpha Phi Omega approached me to join. I accepted the invitation and pledged. It was during the initiation period that I met Dwight Clinton Jones, who would become my best friend and who has been more than a brother. We have spoken to each other at least once a week for the more than 50 years of our friendship. He was in my wedding, and I was in his. We watched our children grow up and our grandchildren come. He preached at my parents' and my brother's funerals and likewise, I his. We have traveled the world, shared our resources, and trusted each other's candid evaluation of the other. It is rare to find a true friendship that endures the test of time, but we have!

In the fall semester of my sophomore year, I met a beautiful and smart young lady, Inez Nunnally. We had a psychology class together where Dr. Samuel Carter was the professor. I sat behind her in class and attempted to pursue a relationship with her. She appeared to initially be uninterested in my pursuit. However, with much persistence, I was able to overcome her reluctance. I often say that she simply could not resist my charm. I must note that this is my version of the story. I am sure she would have another version to share!

Nevertheless, we began to date, and ultimately, I asked her to marry me and she said yes.

The decision to find a mate is among the most important that a person will make. It was certainly very true for a young minister in training during my time. I acknowledge that the expectations and times in which we live today have changed. Yet even today in this extremely tolerant culture, the decision to marry and to whom, or the decision to remain single will have far reaching consequences.

Inez and I exhaustively discussed our anticipated decision and prayed that God would bless our union. He has, and she has become for me a great gift and expression of His grace. Through twisting roads, high mountains, deep valleys, sunshine and rain, laughter and tears, bad times and good, she has helped navigate the way. Her partnership as friend, advisor, mother of our children, and soulmate is inexpressible. She continues to be the most treasured confidant in my life.

During my sophomore year, the civil rights movement was heading to a boil. From 1954 to 1968 the civil rights movement was intensifying. Four little girls died in the bombing of the 16th Avenue Baptist Church in Birmingham, Alabama. The fervor of the movement spread across the south. In Petersburg, a Virginia Union graduate and the pastor of Gillfield Baptist Church, Dr. Wyatt Tee Walker, gave up his pastorate to join the movement as chief of staff of the Southern Christian Leadership Conference (SCLC) under the leadership of Dr. Martin Luther King Jr. Virginia Union students were arrested for protesting at the lunch counter in Tallhimers Department Store.

By 1968, the tensions around race were at an all-time high. I recall walking across campus on April 4, 1968, and hearing that Dr. Martin Luther King Jr. had been shot and killed in Memphis, Tennessee. All over America riots and protests broke out. On VUU's campus that night, a vigil was held in honor of Dr. King. I was asked to give his "I have a dream" speech. I had memorized it for other occasions. It was a moving moment. I can feel the moment even now as I write about it.

That night all of the Black community was searching for grace. I think that Martin Luther King Jr.'s sacrifice caused many to embrace the social implications of the gospel. I know that his life and witness urged me on to become an advocate. Though I never met him, from a distance he modeled for me in my formative years what relevant ministry looks like.

The closest I got to King's ministry was in my freshman year when Dr. Allix James, then dean of the School of Religion, summoned my good friend Dwight Jones and I to pick up Dr. Wyatt Tee Walker from Byrd Field, the Richmond Airport at the time. What enthusiasm overwhelmed us as we anticipated meeting this charismatic preacher from Harlem, NY who had been chief of staff to Dr. King. We were profoundly impressed by his accessibility, insight, and exposure. It was as though we had a front row seat to the civil rights movement as he spoke from his experience. I did not know that later in my career, I would have an opportunity to be mentored by him, and to serve in the same city with him.

When I review this early unfolding of my life through the prism of grace, I am overtaken with an immense sense of grateful emotion. God set me up to achieve!

The Function of Legacy: What Mean These Stones?

THERE ARE TIMES IN THE AFRICAN AMERICAN EXPERIENCE when we pause and celebrate our history—times when we stop to acknowledge the contributions of our ancestors and recognize African heritage and affirm the accomplishments that have been achieved during our plight and our participation in this country. Unfortunately, some of us have missed the real value of legacy, and the importance of understanding where we came from and how we have arrived at where we are. Some of us have such a short understanding of our generational pilgrimage.

Our history and legacy empower us to have high esteem for ourselves. That's why it is important for us to see to it that our children understand our struggle. Too many people today are deprived of an understanding of who they are because the institutions of American society have not fully embraced the contributions of Black people in this country.

Our schools still inadequately tell the story of Black people in America. It is possible for someone to be very smart in America by American standards and not know his or her history.

I had an opportunity to meet with a wealthy young woman who shared many of her global experiences with me, and in the process of our conversation, I just happened to mention W. E. B. Dubois and she didn't know who he was. She didn't know who George Washington Carver was or Booker T. Washington. Now, you may seem shocked by that, but you would be surprised by how many people, Black people in America, don't know who they are nor the representatives of the long struggle of our journey.

It is not because they have purposely chosen not to have a knowledge of these individuals; they have just been left out systemically by the priorities of America's educational system. The priority of America's education system is to perpetuate a false narrative of White superiority and innocence. Many of our schools don't care to call W. E. B. Dubois' name. It is not that this young woman didn't have a good education. Her education was just devoid of her identity and ownership of where she had come from and the contributions of the people that represent her in this American society.

So, when I talk about African Americans, let me clearly run quickly to say that I am really talking about the broad-set concept of what it means to be Black in America. I'm talking about the expanse of Blackness. Some people are caught up in the biracial idea. Some people are "not Black" because their mother is White and their father is Black or vice versa, but let me tell you, in America racism is not a sociological function; it is based in color. If you are any shade of Black, you get treated like you are Black.

We are part of a system in America and in other places throughout the world that has defined the worth of people based on their race, giving many what they believe is a right to treat an entire demographic oppressively because of the color of their skin. Each of us, all of us, have some European in us but you are not penalized because of your European ancestry. You are penalized because you are Black. Black is the reason for our oppression. Blackness was associated with slavery and marginalization—and when you are Black in America and you don't know it, you are confused.

Barack Obama may technically be European and Black, but for American society, he is all Black. So, we need to understand nature and how racism functions in America, so that we can understand our legacy.

When we look at the fourth chapter of Joshua, we see a marvelous statement about the Israelites' sense of legacy and understanding of heritage. As a matter of fact, the entire Old Testament is really a recollection of the legacy and history of the children of Israel. It is how they have sustained their history in the Torah.

As I look at African American history and I think about our young people, I want to make sure that they understand the importance of knowing their heritage and where they came from and have a sense of self-appreciation and self-esteem.

In Joshua, the children of Israel are about to go into the Promised Land. They are about to cross Jordan into the Promised Land. They have been through long years of bondage and wandering but finally, they have come to Jordan and are about to cross over to the Promised Land. But one cannot appreciate the real significance of crossing over to the Promised Land unless one understands that what drove the Israelites to the Promised Land is buried in the life of Abraham.

Abraham said that God told him to go into a land that he would not know, and his ancestors would be blessed to live in the Promised Land. After being lost during all of those years of bondage and persecution, the children of Israel were driven by this historical moment where God promised to take them to the Promised Land. It is their history that informed and caused them to come to their destination. The history of the children of Israel is an important history. After Abraham, Isaac, and Jacob, they were born into slavery under Egyptian captivity and God raised Moses in the house of Pharaoh by Pharaoh's daughter. Moses went to Pharaoh when he became of age and told Pharaoh that God told him to tell Pharaoh to let the Israelites go. Pharaoh ignored Moses and God sent a plague among Egypt, and finally, Pharaoh relented. When he relented, they left the camp of Egypt, but Pharaoh changed his mind and went after them. When he went after them, they had arrived at the Red Sea and God parted the waters and the children of Israel crossed through the Red Sea on dry land. When their enemies pursued them, God caused the Red Sea to close. The Bible says that Pharaoh's army was drowned in the sea.

They found themselves in the wilderness not knowing their way to the Promised Land. They were given a cloud of smoke by day and a pillar of fire by night to guide them and show them the way, and after all that they went through, when they reached the Promised Land, Joshua said, "I want you to build a memorial so that when the children come by, they will ask you, 'What do these mean?' and this will be your occasion to tell them our story."

We as Black people need to tell our story. Our story does not begin with slavery. Our story begins in Egypt. We are not just the sons and daughters of slaves or people taken into bondage from African captivity. We are the sons and daughters of architects, biologists, and scientists who built the pyramids and shaped Egyptian art. If you want to talk about our history, you have to begin in Egypt. You have to begin in ancient civilization. We paused in slavery for a while, along our ultimate progression, but slavery is not our origin nor our destination. We are determined to be free. So, it is today, that just as the children of Israel told their story to their sons and daughters, we must tell the story of our faith and our journey to our sons and daughters. We must make sure that our story is shared because if they do not know the story, they cannot have the competency or the confidence that they need to deal with a world like this.

They need to know how deep and how far their people have come. They need to know that we invented the traffic signal and that a Black man discovered blood plasma and its properties. They need to know that we contributed to this society. They need to know that the whole foundation of America's economy and prosperity was based on the free labor of slaves. They need to know that Black people built the Capitol and the White House. They need to know that we have been engaging in all aspects of America. Black people need to know African American history because it will change our perception of who we see ourselves to be. Our White brothers and sisters need to know African American history because it will change their perception of who we are.

Our story, while it must be told, is not just a collective story. We all have our individual stories—the stories weaving together multiple Black families and Black individuals. Do you know the stories of your forebears? Do you know who and where you came from before you got to the north? Are you in touch with the stories of your great grandparents? Are you in touch with the lineage of your journey? Do you know your story?

It was in writing this book that I first shared the account of how my father left South Carolina, making his way to Baltimore at fifteen years old with no money, limited education, no resources, and no way to figure out how to make it before connecting with my grandfather in Philadelphia, meeting him for the first time.

This story is very important because if my dad had been killed in South Carolina, or become a criminal in Baltimore, I would not be here today preaching the gospel. It is important that we understand our stories and we understand how we arrived at where we are. We must also pass our stories on to future generations, so that they can have some sense of confidence and understand that we have the power to get through because we have been through so much. We are a people who are not timid and fragile and can tell the story of these hard times. Through these stories, we should also understand that we have the ability to maneuver through and overcome the hard times that we encounter still. And, we should understand that we are survivors with a rich heritage that should never be hidden or forgotten and always celebrated and cherished as we continue to walk along the path of grace that God has laid out before us.

CHAPTER FOUR

A Saturday Night Call

IT WAS SATURDAY NIGHT. I WAS IN MY DORM ROOM WHEN a call came from George Langhorne, a student in the Graduate School of Religion at Virginia Union University. I came to know George through our shared interest in ministry. He was an older student who had served in the military and had come to Virginia Union to complete his theological education. At the time, he was also a pastor and had become an early mentor to me.

During the call that night, he said a deacon at the Rising Mount Zion Baptist Church in Fulton had contacted him. Fulton was an economically depressed, historically Black community located in the southeast section of the city. "The church is in crisis," he said. "The minister that they had invited to serve as pastor withdrew from consideration and told them he was not coming." They called the seminary in a panic, searching for a preacher for Sunday morning, but all the graduate students are already committed.

"I told the deacon that none of the graduate students were available, but I did tell him you were, even though you are an undergrad. They're interested if you are," George said.

I agreed to do it.

When Sunday morning arrived, I went to preach. It was clear to the leadership of the church and me that I was not a candidate for the pastorate, given that I met none of the requirements they established for their next pastor. They wanted a man with a graduate degree in theology. He needed to be ordained and have pastoral experience, and they wanted him to be married with a family.

After hearing the list of prerequisites, my pastor jokingly remarked, "Not only do you not meet their requirements, at nineteen you are not even a man." With the understanding that I did not meet the criteria established by the search committee, I agreed to return when invited to preach. As fate would have it, they invited me to return week after week to preach as a non-candidate while the search committee was organizing a new search for a pastor.

What a challenge it was for me, a beginning preacher, to have to preach a new sermon each week to the same people. My minimal sermon reserve was quickly exhausted. I struggled each week to prepare something fresh. I was wonderfully assisted by my then fiancée, Inez, who typed out my manuscript each Saturday night. Meanwhile, I was well received by the congregation each week. After a couple of months, the pulpit committee gave a report to the church on their progress for selecting a pastor to which a member inquired, "Are you considering the young man who has been preaching here on Sundays?"

"No," the committee chair replied. "He doesn't meet the criteria established by the committee."

The member responded, "Can we change the criteria?"

The committee chair shrugged his shoulder and said, "The congregation has the final word."

A motion immediately followed to suspend the criteria and consider me as a candidate. Thirty days later, I was elected pastor of Rising Mount Zion Baptist Church (RMZ).

There I was, a nineteen-year-old teenager and pastor of a 100-year-old congregation. There was some tension among some of the congregation who felt that I was too young, underprepared, and unproven, and objectively, there was much truth in their assessment. Nevertheless, I felt that my selection was an expression of the grace of God.

Moreover, I was too much of a novice to know what challenges lay ahead. One deacon came to me and said, "You cannot be my pastor. I have children older than you." His comments, fortunately, represented the feelings of only a small segment of the congregation. Most of the congregation thought, "Let's give him a chance." To this day, I am truly grateful that they took a chance on me, and I am forever indebted to those who invested in me.

The next move, after being extended the invitation to become pastor, was to become ordained. Ordination was essential to function as a pastor, and it required extensive study to be examined by an ordination council. I asked my pastor back home in Philadelphia to convene a council for my examination. He told me that I would need a coach to assist in my preparation. I asked my friend George Langhorne if he would serve as my ordination coach. He agreed and immediately began my preparation.

George was scholarly and well versed in Baptist doctrine. My pastor gave us two months to prepare to come before the council. Between my classwork and study for ordination, I was overwhelmed. George was there, patient and encouraging, preparing me for examination.

The council was composed of some of Philadelphia's sagest pastors, all experienced and deeply entrenched in Baptist doctrine. They conducted the examination in an open forum before my home church congregation. I sensed that they were praying for me, even as the committee interrogated my familiarity with the material before us. They were very fair and upon completion approved me for ordination with one condition: I would continue my education at the university.

The night concluded with a jubilant worship service and a powerful sermon by George, who admonished me to be faithful and mindful of the investments that many had made in me. By the conclusion of the service, I was overwhelmed by the love of my family, colleagues, and friends.

I returned to Richmond an ordained minister. In my enthusiasm to be acknowledged by other pastors, I put in an application to join the Baptist Ministers Conference of Richmond and Vicinity. My application created a surprising controversy. The dean of Richmond's pastors, Dr. William Lee Ransom, challenged my eligibility. He argued that I was too young to join the conference. His position was that I was still a boy. His colleagues challenged him. They argued that if a congregation had called me and I was ordained, I met the criteria for membership. After some back and forth, the prevailing opinion was that I was eligible for membership. I was voted in as the youngest member of the conference in its history.

Rising Mount Zion was organized in 1869, four years after the emancipation of enslaved Africans, and 100 years later in April of 1969, Rising Mount Zion Baptist Church installed me as pastor. I immediately assumed responsibilities of the pastorate. I started familiarizing myself with my congregation and the people of the community. Rising Mount Zion had a long history in the Fulton community; it was the mother church, and I had become the pastor as the church was celebrating its Centennial Anniversary.

Inez and I were married at the church a year later. Residents lined the streets with jubilation as we rode through Fulton on the way to the reception at the newly constructed Henderson Center on the campus of Virginia Union University.

I will never forget the sense of affirmation I felt when the congregation elected to purchase a parsonage for my bride and me. It was a lovely home and was the family home of a member, Deacon Walter Whiting, a former dean at Bluefield State University in West Virginia.

While the parsonage was being prepared for us, Evelyn and Wilbur Slaughter invited us to live in their home. We lived on the third floor of their home for about four weeks. They were extremely loving to us, and their family was among our most adamant supporters during my tenure as pastor.

A year later, we were blessed with our first child, Orchid. She was not only our delight but was also the joy of the entire congregation. I cannot adequately express how I felt to become a father; it gave me personal purpose. I saw it as another indication of divine favor. We were now a family.

Despite my happily growing family, the challenges of being a new pastor, in a church steeped in revered practices and traditions, were hard to overcome. Some members were reluctant to surrender authority that they had held for a long time, even if it should have been with the pastor. Every pastor must understand that, for the most part, a congregation calls a person to become the pastor not to be the pastor. One does not gain pastoral authority by simply accepting the invitation to serve in the position. Every church has a pastor, but it may not be the one who has the title. Pastoral authority is earned in the crucible of service and in the investment into the lives of those served. Sometimes the earning of authority requires struggle over a period of time, and in some cases, the pastor fails to become the leader, resulting in termination of the pastor's tenure. My time at Rising Mount Zion was filled with leadership tension. There had been a legacy of leadership tension across the years. While I did not enjoy this tension, it helped develop my pastoral insight.

The Fulton community, in many ways, had been isolated from the mainstream of Richmond. It was a Black ghetto with marginalized access to city services. Its real estate was old, yet preserved, and it had been an isolated community within the town when segregation and discrimination had been more prevalent. Over time Fulton inherited a bad reputation among White people and middle-class Blacks as well. It was comprised of a mostly low-income Black population. Many, however, had lived there for generations, and their children had achieved great success, such as Ms. Teresita Braxton, who was the registrar at Virginia Union University for many years, and Samuel L. Gravely Jr., who was the first Black admiral in the United States Navy. By the time I arrived, it was an extremely neglected part of the city of Richmond. It was the perfect place for me to practice the social gospel I admired in the civil rights movement.

Early on, I met the Reverend Joe B. Fleming, pastor of the Quioccasin Baptist Church in Henrico County, and director of the Richmond Community Action Program (RCAP), which advocated for the rights of the citizens of Fulton. We became partners in the struggle for justice and dear friends for life. "Joe B," as he was affectionately called, was an encourager and enabler who worked effectively behind the scenes. He helped to fashion my skills as a spokesman and advocate for the people of Fulton and beyond.

Just as I took on my pastoral responsibilities, the city of Richmond decided to launch an urban renewal project in Fulton, which planned to displace the Black population. In most cities across the country, "Urban Renewal" meant Black removal.

In Fulton, we fought against any Urban Renewal that would displace families who cherished their roots in the Fulton community. Ultimately, we were forced to negotiate a plan that would completely honor the emotional and cash equity that residents had in their homes, whether they were owners or renters. The plan took into consideration the disruption and negative impact on the citizens of the community and fair housing and relocation expenses for homeowners. The citizens participated in the planning, and we disrupted all development activities until our demands were met. In addition to all the socioeconomic challenges that confronted the citizens of Fulton, there were also geographical complications, which impacted the quality of life as well.

Fulton is located at the lowest point in Richmond, along the James River, and is subject to frequent flooding, resulting in a deteriorated dam system. When the river overflowed its banks after a storm, the Fulton community was flooded out. People would be driven out of their homes, schools would be closed, and businesses would be shut down. On one occasion, I led a march from Fulton to the Richmond housing authority, sitting in until we could get housing consideration for displaced residents. We did not leave until they received housing.

Two years into my tenure at Rising Mount Zion, I was invited to preach at Saint James Baptist Church in Varina, a suburban community. My immediate predecessor at Rising Mount Zion, the Reverend James Ealey, had simultaneously pastored Saint James and Rising Mount Zion during his tenure. In July 1971, after preaching several times, the opportunity to serve both congregations was extended to me, as it had been to my predecessor, and I accepted. The congregations had become comfortable with the arrangement of sharing their pastor. One worshiped at 8:00 am and the other at 11:00 am on Sunday. Saint James was not as large a congregation as Rising Mount Zion, but it was a loving congregation. They were dissimilar in that one was urban and the other rural. Saint James had no social or community issues to be addressed, nor was it plagued with a legacy of leadership conflict.

During my time as pastor, I continued my studies part-time, though I was inhibited by the demands of being a dual pastor. I also received a myriad of invitations to preach around Virginia and beyond. I was at the forefront of defending the rights of the citizens of Fulton against the city and the Urban Renewal Agency, further pulling my focus from my college degree.

One day, Inez and I were waiting for a traffic light to change near campus. Dr. Allix B. James, president of the university, pulled up beside us. He waved at us and shouted, "Come up to my house right away!"

Unwilling to spurn the president of the university, we complied. Upon our arrival, he invited us to be seated in the parlor. We exchanged pleasantries, but soon we learned the reason that he had invited us.

"Richardson," he said in a tone that made me sit upright, "I know you are now a successful pastor. You have become a leader in this community. But, you have not completed the requirements for your undergraduate degree. If you fail to complete it, you will always be apologizing for not having it. The longer you wait, the harder it will be. The absence of a degree will compromise your confidence and limit your opportunities."

Before I could say a word, my wife said, "You are right, Dr. James." She turned to me. "I have been telling him the same thing." The double team by the president and my wife was the most meaningful intervention I have ever had. I left the president's house, resolved to finish my degree. Oh, what an act of grace!

With a newfound motivation for completing my degree and an overwhelming sense of support from those around me, I also began to realize that one of the joys of pastoring in Richmond was the great collegiality of the young pastors in the city. We often shared in a rich fellowship. We were drawn together by a common interest to engage our congregations in progressive ministry that was informed by the social gospel, as exemplified in the civil rights movement, and empowered by a theology of social activism. In addition, we found our collaboration helpful as beginning pastors trying to navigate our way through the unknown waters of pastoral leadership. The opportunity to consult each other was invaluable.

Through this cluster of pastors, we organized the first Citywide Revival in the city of Richmond. It was a unifying event for the church community. It was an opportunity that exposed us and the city to nationally acclaimed preachers, such as Hilton James of Brooklyn, Manuel Scott of Los Angeles, and Harold Carter Sr. of Baltimore. Their visits gave us the occasion to partake of their skillful pulpit mastery. During their informal time, we engaged their thinking around the challenges of ministry. They were generous in sharing their insights borne of years of experience.

It was my responsibility to host our guest, which provided me access to a more personal encounter. On a Friday evening, I was invited to preach at Moore Street Baptist

Church. Dr. Manuel Scott Sr. arrived in Richmond two days earlier than the designated schedule to begin the revival. So, I invited him to join me at Moore Street Baptist Church, and he agreed to come. That was a pivotal night in my preaching ministry. I preached the sermon, and after the service concluded, we were driving back to the hotel, when Dr. Scott said, "Rich, that was a good job you did tonight with that sermon." He continued to share his gentle critique of my preaching performance. "Not every preacher has the ability to preach without written notes, but you can. You needed to abandon the manuscript and use the preaching moment as an act of faith, not just preaching faith but actualizing faith in the delivery of the sermon."

I was such an admirer of Dr. Scott and how he preached with power without a script. His comments so impacted me that his advice spoke courage into me and caused me to take the risk. From that night to this, I have not taken a manuscript to the pulpit. I must confess that across the years, there have been times when invited to speak at high profile preaching occasions, I wanted to run and get my prepared, written manuscript. Nevertheless, by the grace of God, I have resisted.

Dr. Scott was not endorsing underprepared extemporaneous babbling. He was calling me as a preacher to greater rigor, organization, prayer, and trust in preparation and in God. His insight and advice has blessed me, but this is not to say that preachers who use manuscripts in the pulpit are less authentic. The preacher must discover what best suits him or her.

In addition to the comradery of junior pastors, senior local pastors who invested their time and insight into our development enhanced our awakening to the broader road of the pastoral role. Dr. G. G. Campbell, Pastor of Moore Street, was such an elder statesman. He invited my best friend Dwight Jones and me to go with him to our first religious convention, The Lott Carey Convention, convening in Harlem, New York, at the Convent Avenue Baptist Church. We arrived in New York excited because not only was it our first convention, it was my first visit to New York City.

Dr. Campbell was a knowledgeable guide. We stayed at the New York Hilton and attended the sessions during the day. One evening, Dr. Campbell suggested we see a play. I did not realize at the time that it would be such a valuable part of our visit to a religious gathering in New York. He demonstrated for us, through his insistence that we see the play, a link between the sacred and the secular. What an essential linkage for a young pastor developing theological formation.

The Broadway show was "Hello, Dolly!" starring Pearl Bailey. It was such an exciting and inspiring production. On the way back to the hotel, Dr. Campbell led us in dissecting the play for its theological application and sermonic illustrative value. We all agreed that the lyrics of the lead song, "Before the Parade Passes By," held the most profound sermonic value of the play. We agreed that the takeaway was that the song spoke of taking advantage of opportunities while you have a chance. Our collective application was that life could be littered with missed opportunities. Each of us returned home that Sunday, incorporating our perspective of the fresh insight gained from our visit to Broadway. The long-term impact of that experience underscored the value of developing a sermonic eye for contemporary illustrations in every aspect of life.

My time as a pastor in Richmond was fulfilling not only because of the social justice advocacy but also the traditional pastoral responsibilities like preaching, counseling, visiting the sick, blessing babies, baptizing the converted, working with youth, and comforting families in time of grief. My time at Rising Mount Zion and Saint James provided the foundation for my future in ministry. It was through the trials and tensions of these two congregations that I learned the skills necessary to navigate the changing ebb and flows of an African American congregation. They equipped me with knowledge I would have never gained in the seminary.

There is a saying that a pastor is like a physician; he or she is a practitioner, learning to be a pastor by being a pastor. What a gift of grace to have had this opportunity for such early exposure to ministry.

CHAPTER FIVE

A Long Shot

ONE OF THE GREAT GATHERINGS OF AFRICAN AMERICAN pastors in Virginia was the annual ministers' conference at Hampton Institute in Hampton, Virginia. Hundreds of African American pastors attended, primarily from up and down the east coast of the United States. Some of the greatest preachers in the country stood at that pulpit in Ogden Hall and mesmerized the attendees with extraordinary oratorical skill and brilliant theological insight. Among the incredible purveyors of the art of preaching were Gardner Calvin Taylor, Sandy Frederick Ray, William Augustus Jones, Samuel Proctor, Miles Jones, and Harold A. Carter Sr. just to name a few.

It was at this conference in June 1974 that my colleague, an extremely popular Richmond, Virginia preacher, the Reverend Benjamin Robertson, pastor of Cedar Street

Baptist Church, asked me, "You've heard of Grace Baptist Church, right? The one in Mount Vernon, New York."

"No, I haven't. Why?"

"The pulpit is vacant." He paused and leaned towards me. "It's a great church. My late friend, the Reverend Shelton Doles, had been the pastor. I've even preached there, and I know some of the leadership. If I were to recommend you, I think they'd take my recommendation. Would you be interested in preaching there?"

I blinked, a little surprised. "I would."

He contacted them, and I received an invitation to preach four weeks later. I was warmly received when I preached at Grace. I returned home, excited about the possibility of being considered in the church's process to select a pastor. I always felt that I had not landed where I would remain. The summer passed, and I did not hear from them. Then in early autumn, I received a call from the pastoral search committee inviting me to return as an official pastoral candidate, and I was also asked to bring my wife.

The prospect of going to New York was exciting and intimidating for both of us. Mount Vernon, New York is a city located in the southern tier of Westchester County, bordering the borough of the Bronx to the south, the city of Yonkers in the north, and the city of New Rochelle in the east. Its Black population began to emerge in the fifties. Before that time, the Black community was composed mostly of domestics who did chores for the upper-middle-class population. By the time I visited Grace, the city of Mount Vernon had a high-density population of about

70,000 people in four square miles. The Black population was approximately fifty percent and growing.

We arrived in New York to the caring hands of Deacon Wallace Williams, who remained our devoted friend until the end of his life. All of the people of Grace were warm and welcoming. They received my sermon with enthusiastic delight. After service, I was invited to a wonderful dinner at the home of Deacon and Mrs. James C. Johnson, the immediate past chairman of the deacons' ministry. After the meal, the search committee interviewed me. The next day we returned home, excited by the prospect that we could be moving to New York.

Meanwhile, I continued to address the needs of my congregation and community. A month after my visit to Mount Vernon, I was contacted by the search committee informing me that, with my consent, they would like to worship at my church. I agreed. They also asked if I would meet after service for an interview. Inez and I invited them to our home for dinner and the interview. They came, and Inez cooked and served a great Virginia meal. She served corn pudding, succotash, collard greens, potato salad, candied yams, ham, fried chicken, yeast rolls, and iced tea. I think the meal was a significant contributor to the impression made that night. They almost forgot to conduct the interview! They left when the evening concluded, and after two long months we were informed that the committee wished to present my name as a candidate for the pastorate along with two other candidates. I consented to be included. I prayed and asked God to guide me in my pursuit as this consideration began. While my hopes were high and I really wanted to become pastor of Grace, I recognized, given the competition, I was a long shot! One of the other candidates had a Ph.D. from Boston and was far more experienced than I. The other had a Master of Divinity from Virginia Union University and many years of pastoral experience. I had yet to finish my degree, and I was only twenty-five.

Despite all that, I was elected Pastor of Grace Baptist Church on January 19, 1975. I learned again that the favor of God could take a long shot or a no shot and turn it into a sure shot. I was the least likely choice, but once again, His grace had covered my inadequacy. What a sense of joy and affirmation I felt that night when the chairman of the deacons called to tell me that I had been called to be the pastor of Grace.

I made several visits to Grace before my family and I officially moved. During one of them, my best friend, Dwight Jones, accompanied me.

"Are you sure you want to move here?" He asked. "The building is practically falling apart."

"I know the building is in bad shape, but you met the people. They have the desire to be great. They have been great in the past, and they expect to be a great church again. I came to Grace because the people have great expectations of themselves." I turned to him and smiled. "I think you're just worried we won't be able to hang out."

Firm in my conviction, it was time to plan my family's transition from the familiarity of Virginia to the complexities of metropolitan New York. The first phase of the transition was to say goodbye to the people of Rising Mount Zion and Saint James, whom I had grown to love and who had grown to love me. The churches planned a farewell service, where expressions of gratitude were exchanged and tears were shared, both theirs and mine.

We left Richmond focused on our future in a completely different place. I was committed to completing my education at Virginia Union, but I trusted the hand of God in my decision to move to New York. I was not intimidated by whatever might lie ahead. One of the early lessons I learned as a person of faith was to surrender the details of the future into the hands of God. Inez, my daughter Orchid, and I drove to Mount Vernon, crossing the George Washington Bridge into our future.

An enthusiastic delegation of members of the congregation received us and attended to every detail of our transition. They assured us that we were welcome by their words and deeds, and they, too, were excited about our future together as pastor and people.

On April 1, 1975, the first Sunday after my arrival, I was presented to the congregation and assumed the full responsibilities as pastor elect. The church was full to capacity. The membership of the church at the time was 429, but on that Sunday, members and non-members alike had come to see the new pastor and his family and to hear the pastor-elect preach his first sermon. The worship service was energizing, and the atmosphere was encouraging to me. Preaching at Grace was initially a weekly challenge as I struggled to remain fresh, inspiring and relevant, an ambition I have tried to sustain all of these years. I officially began my journey at Grace Baptist Church on that morning in the city of Mount Vernon, a journey that would last more than 45 years.

Grace was a much larger congregation than my previous assignment. It took some time and effort to get oriented to the membership, the surroundings, and the broader community, but I hit the ground running. I started by meeting the leadership, deacons and trustees, then small groups, youth and children and their leadership. I was invited to dinners and many social events in the first year. These occasions provided me unofficial, but vital, insight into the culture of the church. I immediately began to assess the strength of the church by looking at its active membership, finances, the condition of the building and its potential, given the surrounding demographics.

After sharing my assessments with the leadership, we agreed on three things we needed to do. First, we needed to launch a stewardship campaign, encouraging each member to become a tither through Bible study, preaching and prayer. Second, we should refurbish the building, including changing the exterior from the dull old brick to a white brick. Third, we needed to expand the footprint of Grace beyond Mount Vernon to the region, through a regional radio ministry and a focus on encouraging members to invite potential new members to attend services and special events. We commenced each of these initiatives during my first ninety days, which were foundational to the life of the church's future.

On the first Sunday in April 1975, I was officially installed as pastor of Grace Baptist Church. Several worship services throughout the week leading up to that day concluded with a grand banquet in New York City. The formal installation on that Sunday marked the official beginning of our time together.

I still had some unfinished business in Richmond to attend to. I had not completed the requirements for my bachelor's degree. It was quite challenging to manage the multiple demands on my life. I was a new pastor in an unfamiliar city needing to become familiar with the people, provide access to the members, and vision for the congregation. In addition, there was a need to provide time for weekly sermon preparation.

There was a community waiting for the continuing engagement of our church in the social dynamics of the city. Add to that, I was a husband, a father, and we were expecting our second child. I had more than enough responsibilities to justify delaying the completion of my degree. But I could not stop rehearsing in my mind what Dr. A. B. James said to me, "If you fail to complete your degree, you will be apologizing for it for the rest of your life." So, I reenrolled at Virginia Union University that September.

To accommodate my pastoral obligations and student assignments, I divided my week: Monday through Thursday afternoon, I was in Richmond at the University. From Thursday evening through Monday morning I would be in Mt. Vernon. Each Monday morning, I would catch a plane from New York to Richmond and return home on Thursday afternoon.

Each Thursday evening, my wife would host a dinner at the parsonage for the deacons. At those Thursday evening meetings, I would teach Bible study and vision with them regarding our future as a congregation. The positive fallout from those sessions was unexpected. The time we spent together built a bond between us and gave them the opportunity to understand and embrace my thinking while giving me the occasion to identify the diversity of their gifts. I then spent the balance of the week carrying out my other tasks as pastor. After a year of commuting, I completed my degree requirements.

My mother and my father decided to make the trip to Mount Vernon to visit us during the weekend of Mother's Day, and I knew my mother was disappointed that I did not participate in my graduation. Just before service began on Sunday, I went into the sanctuary, sat down beside her and presented my degree to her. I was the first in our family to graduate from college. She looked at the degree with an admiring gaze and said, "You've finished college, and you can't even spell your name. Your middle name is not spelled FRANKLIN. It's FRANKLYN." We had a big laugh. I could always count on my mom to keep my humility in check.

Within the first year of our tenure at Grace Church, another affirming gift of grace was afforded us: the birth of our son, William Franklyn Richardson III. I was very grateful to have a son. I found tremendous delight, in the midst of a budding career, watching our children evolve into who they would become.

I inherited a socially conscious congregation at Grace. In 1939, Reverend Millard Levister ran for school board trustee, and was the first Black to run for elective office in Westchester County. The Reverend Samuel Austin, my immediate predecessor, was the first Black to run for Mayor of the city of Mount Vernon. Coupled with my own prior involvement in advocacy and social justice, Grace and I were a perfect fit, and I was excited to continue the legacy of social involvement that my predecessors left for us to carry on.

Less than two years into my pastorate, the Mayor of Mount Vernon, August Petrillo, died, creating a vacancy in the office of Mayor. A day or two after his death, the Reverend Richard H. Dixon invited me to go with him to the home of Madilyn Gill to meet with the Republican leadership to discuss the future of the city. Dr. Richard Dixon, Pastor of Macedonia Baptist Church, was highly regarded throughout the city. He was the city's senior pastor and had impeccable civil rights credentials. He was part of the small delegation that accompanied Dr. Martin Luther King Jr. to Oslo to receive the Nobel Peace Prize in 1964. Dr. Dixon became a dear friend, mentor, and confidant.

Ronald A. Blackwood, an African American, was president of the city council and automatically became acting mayor upon the death of Mayor Petrillo. The visit to Madilyn Gill's house, I learned later, was to discuss how the party could avoid supporting Blackwood for mayor. While I was at the meeting, I heard the leadership say, "Mount Vernon is not ready for a Black mayor." They subsequently passed over him.

I was young and a little radical. I left the confidential meeting and went to the newspaper and told a reporter what the Republicans said. Needless to say, they were upset that I had outed them, but they did not support Blackwood. Consequently, the Black community was outraged. We led a massive voter turnout in support of the Democratic candidate Tom Sharpe, who was also White, in response to the Republicans' statement and actions. Sharpe overwhelmingly won the election, but Blackwood remained loyal to the Republican Party in an attempt to give them the benefit of the doubt.

History, however, repeated itself with the death of Mayor Thomas Sharpe in the fall of 1984. The Republican Party rejected Councilman Blackwood again. This time, Blackwood bolted from the Republican Party and became a Democrat. He ran for mayor in a special election in 1985, becoming the first Black elected mayor in the history of New York State. His victory marked the demise of the Republican Party in the city of Mount Vernon, which to this day, has not re-emerged.

My involvement in the mayoral transitions of the mid-seventies through the mid-eighties represented a fight for the political empowerment of the Black community in the city of Mount Vernon. This was followed by a long struggle for Black representation on the school board, and ultimately in the administration of the Mount Vernon School system, a struggle I led as Pastor of Grace and President of the United Black Clergy in the city of Mount Vernon. All of these battles were against the backdrop of a city in transition.

The emergence of the Black population was advanced by White flight to the suburbs, and those who remained desperately tried to maintain political and economic dominance. The struggles were also fueled by an awakening taking place regionally and nationally as manifested in the civil rights movement and the "Black Power" consciousness of the sixties, seventies, and eighties.

This was a fulfilling season in my career that allowed me to put my understanding of the social gospel, to which I had allegiance, into practice. Moreover, I became a witness to the grace of God in advancing the cause of justice in the life of our community. This observation did not stop with what was happening in Mount Vernon, but I also observed the progress being made by Blacks across America. Black mayors and state and national legislators continued to be elected, more and more Black-owned businesses began to open their doors, and the rise of Blacks in corporate leadership continued. All of this social advancement was a stark contrast to the devastatingly harsh origins of our experience as a people in this nation. Our collective progress was, in fact, an act of grace.

In the fall of 1975, I had an opportunity to attend the Lyman Beecher lecture series at Yale Divinity School (YDS) to hear one of the greatest preachers in the English-speaking world, the Reverend Gardner Calvin Taylor, pastor of the Concord Baptist Church of Brooklyn, New York. That week, Reverend Taylor developed his lectures around the query raised by the Apostle Paul in his writings to the Christians at Rome, "How Shall They Preach?" His message was filled with brilliance, authority, compassion, and biblical familiarity. It was superbly poetic and extremely commutable to the audience. It was delivered efficiently using the tremendous gift of his vocal instrument. I was captured by each word that fell from his lips.

On my way home I dreamed of the unlikely possibility that I could go to YDS to continue my theological education. The very next week I decided to speak with a friend who was a recent graduate of YDS, and he offered to write a letter of recommendation on my behalf.

"You'd be a great fit," he told me. "Besides, your church is only an hour away from Yale."

I shrugged. "I've never been great at school."

"You'll be fine." He pointed to himself. "I graduated. And you've met with Dr. Gardner C. Taylor before, right? If you can get Dr. Taylor to recommend you, your admission is secured." I had met Dr. Taylor several times. He knew of me as the new pastor of Grace in Mount Vernon. When I called him and asked for his assistance in getting accepted to YDS, he was excited by the idea, and I was admitted with a full scholarship.

I enrolled in September 1977. I remember walking across the campus, unbelieving that I was a student at Yale. I wanted to pinch myself to see if I was truly there. I had a hard time reconciling where I was with where I had come from. I had barely been admitted to Virginia Union. Now I was accepted to Yale with a full scholarship, including graduate housing, books, and personal funding. Oh, for the grace of God!

My time at Yale was so helpful, even though by the time I was admitted to seminary I had been preaching every Sunday for ten years. The seminary study enhanced my knowledge of the Bible. In addition, it gave me exegetical skills and tools that deepened the well from which I could draw theological insight and biblical authority.

Another well of pastoral insight came to me shortly after our move to New York. I developed a close bond with Reverend Dr. Sandy Frederick Ray, pastor of the Cornerstone Baptist

Church of Brooklyn, New York, and his wife, Mrs. Cynthia Ray. Mrs. Ray, after discovering that her son and I were classmates at West Philadelphia High School, adopted my wife and I as her children. Our relationship gave me unlimited access to Dr. Ray, who had a legendary career as a preacher, pastor, and national religious leader. He became my mentor. I met him in the last four years of his life. The time I spent with him was very special. He freely imparted so much wisdom when I was in his presence. I have great insights and stories that he shared when we were traveling.

Dr. Ray was sought after all over America. Preachers coveted his sermons in Baptist churches throughout all of the Baptist conventions. He was president of the Empire Baptist State Convention and vice president of the National Baptist Convention when I met him. He served the Cornerstone Baptist Church for more than forty years.

One day while we were sharing, I asked Dr. Ray if he had considered placing some of his sermons in a book for future generations. He was a very humble man and questioned whether his work was worthy of publication. I told him I thought, as a young preacher, that his sermons needed to be available for preachers unborn.

He agreed to let me handle the project. I assured Dr. Ray that I thought Broadman Press would be open to publishing a book of his sermons. I contacted Broadman Press, and they were enthusiastic about the prospect of the publication. Dr. Ray gave me power of attorney, and I went to Nashville to negotiate the terms of the contract. I organized the sermons he selected with the assistance of Ms. Walls, his secretary. I sent them to Nashville and went to Broadman to pick up the galley and brought them to Brooklyn for his approval. After his approval, I returned them to the publisher.

One evening I had just completed Bible study. It was just one week after returning Dr. Ray's page proofs when a call came informing me that Dr. Ray had died. I immediately went to Brooklyn to be with Mrs. Ray. In the days leading up to the funeral, I assisted her with planning the details for the celebration of Dr. Ray's life. During this time, she asked me to bring the ministers' tribute. I pushed back saying, I was honored by her asking, but I felt that I had not reached the status to speak on behalf of all the great pastors across the nation who had known and loved Dr. Ray. I will never forget her stern response, "Franklyn, do you not know the power of a moment? You will do what I've asked."

I spoke at the service, reflecting on the material in his book, entitled *Journey Through the Jungle*, that only I had access to and had not yet been released.

At the close of the funeral service, Dr. T. J. Jemison, general secretary of the National Baptist Convention, who had visited Grace as a guest preacher at my invitation, came to me and commended me on the tribute I gave. He apparently saw or sensed my grief.

"You lost your mentor today," he said.

I pressed my lips together, "Yes I did."

"Don't worry," he said, "I'm going to take his place." Later I would come to know the significance of those words. And, I remembered the question Mrs. Ray asked me, "Do you not know the importance of a moment?"

I have benefited from mentoring my entire career. I learned early on the value of merging youthful ambition with seasoned wisdom. I welcomed Dr. Jemison's offer and cultivated it as I had with earlier mentors. Among them were my pastor Reverend James Hamlin, State Senator Freeman Hankins, President Allix Bledso James, Foreign Mission Secretary Reverend William Harvey III, and Dr. Wyatt Tee Walker. Once one gets to a place in life where you no longer have mentors, this is an opportunity to mentor those following you. This is where I am today. Each of us owe a debt to the past, to which we should pay the future.

I have learned, as a pastor, that the role of mentoring is a fundamental function. It requires personal investment, uncompromising integrity, critical assessment, and sincere counsel. It may be over a sustained period or for just a season in the life of another. Those who I have had occasion to mentor have blessed me as they have sought my counsel.

There was a time in the Black church when the normal vehicle for receiving the legacy of ministry in preparation for the pastorate was through intergenerational sharing. Clergy today would do well to reflect on the renewal of the vitality of that practice.

My father and mother, the late William Franklyn Richardson and Amanda Florine Ellison Richardson were the parents of three children. I, William (W.) Franklyn Richardson II, am their first child. I was born into a family steeped in the body of Christ.

W. Franklyn Richardson elementary school photo.

This is my elementary school photo. My memoir herein is written to chronicle my life as a "Witness to Grace."

My brother Ronald Richardson was the second child to join our family and my sister Vickilyn Richardson Reynolds is the youngest.

I began my matriculation at Virginia Union University in Richmond, Virginia in 1967 and was elected freshman class president by my peers.

Second from left, I was elected vice president of the Student Government Association during my sophomore year.

W. Franklyn Richardson, 2nd from left, vice president of Student Government Association.

W. Franklyn Richardson left of Muhammad Ali during his 1968 visit to VUU campus.

Left of Muhammad Ali, I escorted the heavy weight boxing champion during his visit to Virginia Union University.

Serving communion at my second of two pastorates, St. James Baptist Church. I was licensed and ordained as a minister while matriculating at VUU.

I met the love of my life in our psychology class at Virginia Union University. Subsequently I proposed and she said, "Yes."

This year we will celebrate our 50th year of marriage.

Inez and I are pictured here at our wedding reception in the Thomas Henderson Center at Virginia Union University following our June 6, 1970 wedding at Rising Mt. Zion Baptist Church where I served as pastor.

We came to Grace Baptist Church in 1975 with our daughter Orchid.

Our family grew with the birth of our son William Franklyn Richardson III.

Here I am pictured with my friend and colleague the Reverend Jesse Louis Jackson Sr. who regularly preached at Grace. He was my installation banquet speaker in 1975 and my 10th Pastoral Anniversary speaker in 1985.

Here with my dear friend and mentor the late Bishop John Hurst Adams, Senior Bishop of the African Methodist Episcopal Church and chairman of the Conference of National Black Churches.

Here I am with Dr. Martin Luther King Sr. who preached at Grace Baptist's 90th Church Anniversary.

My 1975 installation banquet as Pastor of Grace Baptist Church in Mt. Vernon. Left to right: The Reverend Jesse Louis Jackson, banquet speaker, the Reverend W. Franklyn Richardson, Dr. Richard H. Dixon, actor Ozzie Davis, and Deacon Ozzie Reuben.

Dr. & Mrs. Jemison with Inez and I at the National Baptist Convention in New York, 1993.

Dr. T. J. Jemison, David N. Dinkins, mayor of city of New York, and I, 1993.

Dr. Richardson led delegation from National Baptist Convention, USA to Ethiopia in 1984 to bring famine relief during the country's most severe famine.

I led a delegation from the National Baptist Convention, USA, Inc. to Ethiopia in 1994 during the most severe famine in the country's history.

Here with my best friend, the Reverend Dwight C. Jones, and colleague and friend, the Reverend Boise Kimber.

Dr. Wyatt Tee Walker hooding me with the doctoral of ministry as a Wyatt Tee Walker, Fellow at United Theological Seminary, Dayton, Ohio, 1997.

I, along with street soldiers, protested to get out the vote for the sake of our children. Education is the key!

Grace Baptist Church's African American Men's Conference empowering men to be knowledgeable about challenging issues facing us.

CHAPTER SIX

The Birth of Global Consciousness

FRESH FROM THE DOMESTIC CONSTRAINTS OF MY HOMETOWN in Philadelphia and my initial pastorates in Virginia, I was confronted with a view of an expanded horizon. There was an awakening beginning in me, a global consciousness.

In May 1976, a year after coming to New York, Dr. Wyatt Tee Walker invited Inez and me to travel to Brazil with Dr. William Augustus Jones, Pastor of Bethany Baptist Church in Brooklyn, and his wife, Natalie Jones, along with Jimmy Walker, Wyatt's brother, under the escort of Moses Hanania, owner of Consolidated Tours in Atlanta, Georgia. We accepted the invitation and waited in enthusiastic anticipation for the day of our departure.

The trip to Brazil marked the beginning of a long journey of international travel that would carry me across six continents and more than sixty countries. My global excursions gave me an enlightened worldview. It expanded my understanding of God, of myself and of people of all colors, languages, and faiths. My ministry would have been vastly different if it had been devoid of my global encounters. Travel broadened my window of understanding of creation. Moreover, it made history come alive before my eyes. Brazil was my initiation into a restricted fellowship of international travelers. Inez and I looked at each other in our naiveté and said, "Can you believe we are going across the equator to another continent?"

One of the things we observed upon arriving in Rio de Janeiro was that only dark-skinned people were doing the manual jobs. They were the porters, custodians and maids, keeping the airport clean. There before us was a vivid illustration of global racial oppression.

I was greeted by the harsh reality that racism is a global challenge. I traveled 4,000 miles to see a replica of what I had encountered in the United States. While racism is the original sin of the United States of America, its origins are found in other parts of the world. It is a transnational sin, born of greed for wealth and power.

Americans often approach racism from the origins of enslavement, marked by the twenty-plus enslaved Africans who arrived on a Spanish slave ship in 1619 at Port Comfort, Virginia. It was the beginning of cruel treatment of African men, women, and children in America. I contend that the date does not go back far or broad enough, in terms of slavery's geographical footprint. History points out that the degenerative values of America were demonstrated in its treatment and genocides of the native people of America, long before its racist implementation of the enslavement of Black people. In addition, at the seat of global racial oppression is the White Christian church; Great Britain, The Netherlands, Spain, Portugal, and the United States are all co-conspirators to nearly 500 years of African global slavery.

Mary Elliott and Jazmine Hughes described the church's involvement in *The 1619 Project*, published by The New York Times. "The Roman Catholic Church in the fifteenth century divided the world in half in its quest for land and gold. It granted Portugal a monopoly on trade in West Africa and Spain the right to colonize the New World. Pope Nicholas V buoyed Portuguese efforts and issued the Romanus Pontifex of 1455. It affirmed Portugal's exclusive rights to territories it claimed along the West African coast, including the proceeds of the trade from those areas. It granted Portugal the right to invade, plunder, and reduce persons to perpetual slavery."

I saw the results of this especially clearly as our group continued from Rio to the northeastern state of Bahia to its capital city of Salvador, where, in times past, Africans were sold and enslaved against their will. Salvador is known for its historical center where the memory of slavery in Brazil is alive. We heard the stories of our forebears, saw artifacts from the enslavement period, and visited the bush area where slaves were housed. It is sacred ground.

While traveling throughout Brazil, I could see and sense the African cultural heritage of the people in their music, dance, skin color, and diet. Brazil was a wonderful prelude to the global journey that awaited me. It focused my lens, heightened my sensibilities, and made me not merely a tourist, but an observer of the socio-political fabric of each country I would visit.

My next international adventure was at the invitation of the Foreign Mission Board (FMB) of the National Baptist Convention USA, Inc, headed by the Reverend William J. Harvey III. As secretary he was extremely committed to the work of missions. One could feel his passion for the job immediately upon encountering him. The board organized teams of pastors annually to visit mission sites stationed across the African continent. These visits meaningfully impacted those of us who traveled to the mission field.

In the winter of 1980, I had the pleasure of being a member of a team of pastors that included the Reverend Dwight C. Jones and the Reverend Roscoe Cooper, both of Richmond, Virginia, the Reverend Clifford Johnson of Baltimore, Maryland, and the Reverend John Corbett of Greenwood, South Carolina. We embarked on a three-week journey to the motherland, which began in Liberia and included Malawi and Swaziland.

I shall never forget the sense of jubilation I felt when the plane touched down on the African Continent, in Monrovia, Liberia. It was as though I could feel the embrace of my ancestors, and my spirit felt reconciled to my past. That moment was a gift of grace. It was as though God had reserved that day for me from the moment of my birth. My soul danced!

Liberia was an appropriate introduction to the continent, given its history of being populated by African Americans who chose to return to Africa to create an independent nation. It represented one of the responses of enslaved Africans to slavery: the option to leave the continuing fallout of American slavery and return to their native land.

While in Liberia we went out into the bush, to the deep rural interior of the country. We boarded open Range Rovers early in the morning, making our way into the bush to visit one of the mission sites. The trip was long and slow, driving on the rugged red clay roads in the sweltering heat. As we continued deeper into the interior, it felt as though we had abandoned civilization. We saw no signs of community. The deeper we traveled, the more uncomfortable I became. There was nothing familiar left. I had grown up in Philadelphia.

Covered in the red dust of the journey, to the extent that we looked like strangers to each other, we arrived at the village. One of the native pastors at the village, a short man with a clergy collar, greeted us on the road as we disembarked. After shaking my hand, he looked right through to my heart. He could sense my feelings of abandonment and isolation. He smiled at me and said, "Comba bi nea." I blinked and looked at the translator. "God is here!" The translator said.

Despite what appeared to my physical sight to be abandonment, he assured me, though far from the bright lights of American civilization, I had not gone beyond God's reach. The greeting by my African brother was extremely comforting and has continued to be a gift as I have traveled the world. Deep in the bush of Liberia, I learned a lesson that has been instructive wherever I go or whatever I go through. *God is here!* What a gift of grace to know and to experience that God is always present. God does not have to come from anywhere to get to where we are because we can never be absent from Him.

Our visit to Liberia was filled with authentic encounters. Our missions in Liberia were essentially to establish schools to educate the children of the native communities while advancing Christian values. We had the opportunity to meet teachers and students, learning how the investment of our churches were impacting and making a difference in the lives of the people of this third-world nation.

We had an audience with the President of Liberia, the Honorable William Tolbert. Having been in the country for several days, we could feel the unrest in the streets when we traveled to the president's house in government vehicles. Citizens spat on the vehicles in protest of the Tolbert administration. The Tolbert family had a display of wealth, resented by the commoners who were scratching for survival. Less than three months after our visit, April 21, 1980, a military-led coup took over, killing Tolbert and his family. The affairs of Liberia highlighted the fact that people ultimately rebel against oppression regardless of the skin color of the oppressor.

After visiting three other mission schools, we concluded our visit to Liberia. We gained fresh insight into the vital needs our convention was trying to meet in a country with greatly minimized resources. We spent two nights rejuvenating for the journey ahead to Malawi.

The National Baptist Convention sponsored a large school and orphanage in collaboration with the sizeable local fellowship of Baptist churches. The purpose of our trip was to visit the mud hut churches of Malawi. Visiting Malawi put us face to face with the consequences associated with extreme poverty. It raised our sensitivity to their misery and our resolve to assist those who live in these challenging circumstances. Exposure to these countries awakened in me a consciousness I could not have known without international travel.

Our visit included an opportunity to meet with the President of Malawi, Hastings Banda, a physically small gentleman. At the time of our visit in 1980, he had been president since 1966. He served in that position for 28 years. Malawi had been a monarchy, and President Banda governed as a king, suppressing any potential opposition to his rule. He was politically feared yet embraced by the populous as a father figure. Our conversation with him was mostly polite without any discussion of the economic state of the country. He thanked us for the National Baptist Convention's presence and investment in his country.

We exchanged pleasantries and presented him with a gift, as was the expectation. We departed, thankful for having the occasion to have had an audience with the President of this small African nation.

I was overwhelmed by the grace of God manifested in my life, contrasted by the lives of my sisters and brothers in Malawi. The view of others' struggles for existence, seen through the prism of the experience of the Malawians, raised my sensitivity to their desperate plight. The words of John Bradford rang true, "There but for the grace of God go I." It is important to mention that the Malawians, fighting every day for their existence, were enthusiastic about their faith and exhibited great jubilation in their praise and worship. Their worship defied their mud hut context. It was authentic, full of joy and expressions of gratitude in the face of their extremely limited resources. They have authentic gratitude for the gift of life.

When it was time for offering, they lined up and danced up to an offering table, placed a coin, and preceded to repeatedly dance back to the table, placing another single coin. The atmosphere was electric, and their spirit was contagious. They exhibited profound gratitude in their opportunity to praise God for what He meant in their lives. This was clearly the height of the worship experience. They expressed exuberance for the grace of God! The experience was somewhat indicting to those of us who had so much more than they had and whose praise was mild in comparison.

Before our departure from Malawi, we left most of our clothing, personal items, and cash, sharing it with local pastors, who were grateful beneficiaries of our generosity. I remember one Malawian pastor who was given a suit from a member of our delegation. Malawians are short, small people. The pastor giving the suit said, "This suit is too big for you." The Malawian pastor replied, "It be fitting." He was so anxious to receive the suit that he did not want it denied because it did not fit.

For us, it was a feeble attempt to unite in solidarity with their plight. Their struggle with scarcity convicted us to confront our own excessive abundance. It is a wonderful awareness of grace received that awakens generosity in one's heart. Knowing how we were blessed solicited a response of gratitude from each of us. We left Malawi to continue on to the Kingdom of Swaziland, but I will forever be touched by the sincerity of the people of Malawi, awakened to heightened consciousness regarding the poor and neglected, a feeling replicated in all of the mission sites we visited.

The final stop on this mission tour was the Kingdom of Swaziland. Swaziland is a small landlocked monarchy in southern Africa with a population of approximately 1.2 million. It is predominately a Christian nation. It was not as poor as the other mission stations we visited, but there were great needs, largely due to its geographical isolation. Our mission in Swaziland existed primarily of an elementary school. Swaziland was a different window into the diversity within the African culture, in that it was dominated by a king. I did not feel that we had access to the indigenous population in Swaziland. Nevertheless, it did make a contribution to my developing profile of the African continent.

I returned home from my first global journey in February of 1980, and after just one month of returning home, I led a delegation from our congregation to the Holy Land in Israel and Jordan. It was the first of many delegations I would lead abroad. I was joined by my wife, several leaders of our congregation, and a host of other church members. It was an important trip because it brought into focus the actual historical origins and context of Christian faith.

Upon arriving in Israel, we began our journey through the land of the Bible. I had spent my life engaging the scriptures, but nothing illumined them like walking the roads of Israel or visiting the places where the life of Jesus unfolded. I recall visiting the empty tomb and imagining resurrection Sunday, overtaken by a sense of awe.

There is nothing quite as impacting in my travels, as a person of faith, as coming face to face with the empty tomb in the garden, even though before I left New York, to travel six thousand miles to Jerusalem, I knew He was not there because I had already met him in Philadelphia as a youth. Yet, to see the place of His entombment spoke to my faith afresh. "He is not here but is risen, as He said."

Early one morning, we boarded a boat and began crossing Lake Gennesaret, or Galilee, the place where Jesus walked on water and spoke to the wind and the waves. We stopped in the middle of the lake and had a morning devotion. In the quiet of the sea, informed by the scriptures, we visited in our minds what it must have been like when Jesus was there.

My visit to Israel was important from its biblical perspective, but it was also important because it exposed me to the political challenges facing the region. My travel agent, Moses Hanania, with whom I established an enduring friendship until his recent death, was a Christian Palestinian who became an American citizen. He gave me a firsthand understanding of the plight of Palestinians in the region.

Historically, the Holy Land with Jerusalem at its center is significantly sacred to three major world religions: Christianity, Judaism, and Islam. There is a historical struggle between these three world faith communities that is seated in ancient biblical history, far too complex for me to cover in this writing. But, suffice it to say that I found in my first of many visits to Israel a continuing tension between these religions that has resulted in military conflict over occupation of the land historically and more recently since the establishment of the state of Israel on May 14, 1948. Israel, being a strong ally of the USA, has been the dominant force in the region, while, at least, during the same time the Palestinians have experienced grave oppression and discrimination.

Given the history of discrimination and oppression of my own people in America, I have felt and continue to feel some kinship to their plight. To this day, the Christians in Palestine are in threat of extinction. Hopefully the two-state solution will prevail, where Israelis and Palestinians can coexist.

There would be many trips abroad that would follow these initial journeys, but these launched my global pathway and expanded my contextual horizon. These three global contexts provided a sociological, ethnic, and religious perspective by which I viewed the world in my future international encounters.

CHAPTER SEVEN

Aspiration

DR. WILLIAM J. HARVEY III WAS SECRETARY OF THE FOREIGN Mission Board (FMB), the missions department of the National Baptist Convention. Dr. Harvey was both an icon and sage in the affairs of the NBC. He had served more than twenty years as secretary and was a loyal member of the cabinet of President Joseph Harrison Jackson. The National Baptist Convention was the largest African American organization in the world, with over eight million members, and Dr. Jackson led NBC with a strong fist, supported by extremely loyal followers.

I grew up in a church that was a member of the NBC that had a pastor who was a staunch supporter of the Convention and its president. While growing up, I often heard Dr. Jackson's name spoken with the highest esteem. He was considered, among many in his era, as the president of Black America, as well as one of the most brilliant pulpit orators. His preaching was scholarly, captivating, entertaining, and compelling.

Dr. Harvey provided accountable leadership and demonstrated deep commitment to the work of missions which created strong support for him among pastors across the country, both young and old. His result-focused approach to missions drummed up support from among the younger pastors of the denomination. I, in particular, was one of those young pastors.

As we concluded the mission across the African continent, en route from Johannesburg to New York, I found myself in conversation with Dr. Harvey on the plane. I was probing him to gain his insight about the history and future of the Convention. He had a wealth of information about the NBC, and I was glad to receive it.

Early on, I aspired to be president of the National Baptist Convention. I remember standing outside my dormitory, Huntley Hall, at Virginia Union University in my freshman year, sharing my ambition with my classmates. So, I took this opportunity to ask Dr. Harvey, "What is the pathway for a young preacher to rise in the life of the Convention."

"I think," he started, "such a young man would do well to align himself with the future leadership of the convention. The next president will likely be T. J. Jemison of Baton Rouge, Louisiana. He is the general secretary of the Convention. His father was the late Dr. D.V. Jemison, the president of the Convention before Dr. Jackson. You should reach out to Jemison and invite him to your church. He's a Virginia Union man like you. I'm sure he would accept the invitation."

The advice given to me that day became the foundational methodology of my advance to leadership opportunity in the NBC. I had already met Dr. Jemison at Dr. Sandy Ray's funeral and had been acknowledged by him. Immediately upon returning to New York, I wrote a letter inviting Dr. Jemison to be our guest speaker for the 92nd Church Anniversary of Grace Baptist Church, November 2, 1980. He accepted our invitation and came to Mount Vernon.

The word was out that Dr. Jemison was going to challenge the unbeaten Dr. J. H. Jackson. Aware of the rumor, my wife and I hosted a dinner at the parsonage and invited several pastors from the New York area to come and meet Dr. Jemison. It was a warm gathering, and Dr. Jemison shared his vision for the future of the National Baptist Convention. He spoke, indicating that he had not declared his candidacy yet. However, he did answer the questions of those gathered, and all were delighted to be in his presence. The next morning, he preached at Grace and was well received.

A month or so after his visit to Mount Vernon, I received a letter from Dr. Jemison thanking my wife, the Grace family, and me for our hospitality. He also invited me to preach at the church he pastored, Mount Zion First Baptist Church of Baton Rouge. Dr. Jemison and Mrs. Jemison were great hosts. I was treated like royalty on this first of many visits that I would make to Baton Rouge. He enlisted my assistance in securing support among young pastors for his yet-to-be-announced candidacy. I accepted his assignment.

I returned to New York, and we frequently spoke on the progress of his plan. He shared that he was running for president of the Louisiana State Baptist Convention, and if he won that position in July, he would then declare his candidacy. He won, and a few weeks later, he announced his candidacy in Dallas, Texas, with his longtime friend and legendary preacher, Dr. C. A. W. Clarke of Good Street Baptist Church, standing beside him. For the next forty days, the campaign was in full gear! I contacted and solicited support from pastors up and down the eastern seaboard.

All roads led to Miami Beach, Florida, where the convention was being held at the Miami Beach Convention Center. The Jemison Campaign was not allowed to get space in the headquarters hotel, the Fountain Blue, so we held our rally on that Monday night at the Eden Roc Hotel next door. Our crowd was beyond the capacity of the space provided. There were so many people that Dr. Jemison had to stand on a table on the balcony, which I held to assure his safety, to address those gathered. Our campaign truly had exceptional momentum!

The next day was the board meeting where the procedures for the election were to be spelled out. It was rumored that the incumbent, Dr. Jackson, and his team would seek to block the election from going forward. The board meeting was packed to capacity. Many people were approaching the microphones to speak. We intended to get Dr. Jemison's name placed in nomination and ensure that the election would take place.

I will long remember when I approached the mic and said, "My name is W. Franklyn Richardson—"

Before I could finish, Dr. Jackson, President of the Convention, was presiding and said, "I know who you are, and I know your mission here." After much back and forth, we set the procedure and the time of the election.

Thursday morning the election was held and continued all day as each state's delegation went into the voting area and the delegates were individually counted. When the total count was complete, Dr. Jemison had won three to one. The auditorium filled with celebration at the announcement of the election results.

The next morning my wife and I met Dr. Jemison, Mrs. Jemison, and his team for breakfast. Dr. Jemison walked past me over to my wife and asked her, "How does it feel to be the wife of the next general secretary of the National Baptist Convention?" The surprise on Inez's face was only surpassed by the surprise on my face. Later that morning, Dr. Jemison presented my name to the Convention to follow his twenty-nine-year tenure as general secretary. I was elected by a unanimous vote. All the phases of my life were filled with opportunities for growth, but this one surpassed them all.

During the next six months, I lived in a fog. At the age of thirty-two, it was hard for me to believe that I was the general secretary of the largest Black organization in the United States of America. It took some adjustment on my part to take on my new assignment.

I can hardly explain how it felt to be lifted to such a high place of service among the more than 20,000 pastors, most of whom were older than my father. It was a huge undertaking, especially when many felt I was too young to be in such a coveted position. I returned to New York at the close of the session to an exuberant congregation, whose encouragement met me that day and continued throughout the fourteen years of my tenure as general secretary.

The first year as secretary had some turbulence and crosswinds, primarily precipitated by my novelty of the responsibility and unclear expectations, coupled with the president getting adjusted to the expectations of his new responsibilities and defining a clear vision for the denomination. He was obviously more prepared for his new role than I was for mine. His father before him had been president of the Convention, which gave him tremendous insight into the network of the organization. His long tenure as secretary had defined the role for that position, and only he understood the parameters of how it functioned. Initially, with little direction from him, I had to navigate my way, often bumping against the unidentified boundaries.

I became lost because I did not know what was expected of me, and the president reluctantly released the responsibilities that he had executed as secretary. The new national visibility that I received needed to be managed. I was invited to a rally in Chicago, Illinois, where the Reverend Jesse Jackson announced his 1984 candidacy for president of the United States. We were friends; he was the keynote speaker at my installation banquet as pastor of Grace Baptist Church in 1975.

I was included in a photograph at the announcement which included Reverend Jackson, Andrew Young, who was ambassador to the United Nations at the time, Harold Washington, mayor of Chicago, and others. After learning that I was in Chicago at the occasion and seeing my photo in the paper, Dr. Jemison wrote a very harsh letter reprimanding me for attending the rally and for implying, by my presence, the endorsement of the Convention. He went on to say that there were pastors who felt he had made a mistake in making me secretary, but that was not his view. To say that the letter was unsettling would be the understatement of the century. After much prayer and several rewrites, I responded. I sent three copies of my letter by regular mail, special delivery, and certified mail to him. He never acknowledged my response. I still have the letters to this day.

Months later, we had another clash. It was the afternoon before the opening of our first convention, September 1983, in Los Angeles, California. Dr. Jemison assembled the executive officers of the Convention to what I interpreted as a follow-up to his concerns about my appearance in Chicago. He gave me a verbal lashing unequaled to any I had ever received from my father. I left the meeting and went to my room, fell on my knees, prayed and asked the Lord, "If you want me to stay in this position, give me the strength and show me the way." I was humiliated.

I left those episodes determined to study Dr. Jemison, to know his expectations and how he thinks, and to assure him of my loyalty, a decision that allowed me to evolve into his most trusted colleague and personal friend. Mrs. Jemison became my secret confidant in times of controversy. My wife, children, and I came to feel like family to the Jemison family, even spending time with them during holidays and family events.

Once rising from the lowest stage of our relationship, we grew into true partners. I learned so much from both his life experiences and his knowledge of the National Baptist Convention. I was like a sponge absorbing all I could. He advised me as a father to a son. He was generous and became my greatest advocate, placing me on coveted assignments and giving me unprecedented exposure. The personal wisdom he shared was obvious to me, passed on from a collective pool of generational wisdom. Things as detailed as, "Always be prompt; value another's time," and when leaving a hotel room, he would say, "Character is when you cut off the lights when you leave the room, even though you don't have to pay the bill."

I was also informed by his behavior early in our relationship. When traveling, we often shared a hotel suite. One night, after we had said good night and gone to our rooms, I passed by his room later, and the door was slightly opened. I looked in and saw him on his knees beside his bed, praying. It made an impression on me that here was the head of the denomination closing out his day in the privacy of his room, going to the source of his strength. Dr. Jemison was not a perfect man, but he was an authentic Christian.

Dr. Jemison was also a walking encyclopedia on the history and affairs of the National Baptist Convention. He was general secretary in a pre-computer era, but he could rattle off the name, address, and pastor's name of any church of the more than 10,000 registered congregations in a moment's notice. I took it upon myself to learn the same.

During the thirteen years I served as secretary, he shared exhaustive details about the Convention's history, far more than I could retain. I knew as I was listening that I was receiving precious information. He did not just know the history; he had lived it for more than sixty years. He had received the oral history that preceded his time. How I wish he could have completed the book he intended to write. I am thankful that he shared a glimpse of the rich well of his journey in his autobiography, "The T. J. Jemison Story."

The national climate during Dr. Jemison's years as president of the Convention were mixed with progress and pain for African Americans. During those years we sought to use the Convention as a vehicle for Black advancement. One of the greatest challenges facing the National Baptist Convention today is that it has lost its memory. It is disconnected from its past, a noble history full of outstanding leaders, committed to Christ and the church. Those great leaders passed on a legacy of competence, sacrifice, and faith.

One of the things which distinguished Dr. Jemison from his predecessor, Dr. Jackson, was his involvement in the civil rights movement. Dr. Jemison was a founding member and was elected the first secretary of Southern Christian Leadership Conference (SCLC) under the leadership of Dr. Martin Luther King Jr. Dr. King acknowledged in his memoir that he received "invaluable" advice from Dr. Jemison for the Montgomery Bus Boycott, given the fact that he had conducted a successful boycott in Baton Rouge a year earlier. Dr. Jemison was an activist and civil rights leader in Louisiana, as opposed to his predecessor who was socially passive. The civil rights leaders of that era were polar opposites to Dr. Jackson, who was essentially a preserver of the status quo.

Dr. Jemison told me he chose to withdraw from visible national participation so as not to give Dr. Jackson a reason to short circuit his ambition to become president of the NBC.

From the very beginning of his leadership as president, Dr. Jemison signaled that he would be leading the Convention in a different direction. To that end, he invited leaders of the civil rights movement to speak before the Convention at its annual sessions, including Coretta Scott King, C. T. Vivian, Andrew Young, John Lewis, and Reginald Lafayette.

In addition, he communicated where he stood regarding the accomplishments of Dr. King when he led the Convention to donate the statue of Martin Luther King Jr. in 1984 that stands at the entrance of the King International Chapel at Morehouse College. His activism as a civil rights leader and his reputation made the Convention attractive to many young pastors who previously had little regard for the NBC.

Dr. Jemison, in the later years of his career, developed a discomfort with flying, even though he had flown to Europe and Africa in earlier years. While president, he only flew domestically.

As a consequence, he assigned me to represent the denomination in international affiliations. My first assignment was in 1983 with a delegation to Taiwan. It was a multi-denominational delegation of African American church leaders. Our representatives included the late Henry Gregory, Frank Tucker of the District of Columbia, Henry Lyons of Florida, and me. We were guests of the Taiwanese government, an initiative designed to build bridges to Black people in the United States. It was impressive to meet with the heads of state of the people of Taiwan. Their hospitality was superb.

The visit to Taiwan was followed by an assignment to represent the NBC at the General Assembly of the World

Council of Churches (WCC) convening in Vancouver, Canada. I was joined on that assignment by the president of the Women's Auxiliary of NBC, Dr. Mary Olivia Ross. Dr. Ross was a graceful, strong leader of women. She, being my senior, was steeped in the great history of our denomination with years of service in it. I loved "Mother Ross." She was an encourager. We attended all of the sessions and gave valuable input to the ecumenical dialogue from the Black American church perspective. Subsequently, I was elected to the central committee of the World Council of Churches with cross-denominational endorsement.

We subsequently reported the actions and recommendations of the WCC to the annual session of the NBC. The report titled "The Richardson, Ross Report of the World Council of Churches" was well received by the delegates at the annual session. While the World Council only assembles every seven years, the central committee, the governing body of WCC, meets annually, which meant as a member of the central committee, I would attend the governing board meeting in different countries each year. It was tremendous exposure to the church and its issues from a global perspective.

The WCC represented 400 million Christians from 150 countries around the world. The exchange was always rich. It was in this forum that I developed an understanding of and a heart for ecumenism. My membership on the central committee took me to several countries where I had the opportunity to interact with other multiethnic denominations in their context. My journey began in Geneva, Switzerland, at the WCC headquarters, accompanied by Inez and Dr. Ross. The experience of visiting the world center, with its multicultural, multilingual vibe, was fresh and exciting to us. It fostered my evolving global consciousness. The meetings were informative and mentally expanding.

The following year I attended the meeting in Argentina accompanied by my family. In addition to attending the meetings, I had an occasion to preach at several churches. Likewise, the next year Inez and I had an opportunity to attend the central committee meetings in Moscow. I preached at underground churches in Moscow, Russia, a part of the former Soviet Union. The government did not permit the practice of religious worship. However, the presence of the underground churches kept the faith alive. It was powerful to be able to share with those experiencing religious oppression yet holding on to their faith in Jesus Christ. My relationships on the WCC Central Committee and exposure to communions have fueled my abiding interest in ecumenism.

CHAPTER EIGHT

Pathway to Opportunity

In 1984, Ethiopia experienced one of the most severe famines in its history. Thousands were dying from starvation and the lack of medical supplies. The portrait of destitution and starvation were displayed across the national networks in America. This catastrophe was experienced by a Black nation, and wealthy nations were not responding urgently to the crisis. In January of 1984, Dr. Jemison mobilized the churches of the National Baptist Convention to raise funds to eliminate the suffering among the people of Ethiopia. The NBC raised more than 1.5 million dollars to aide in the recovery of those affected by this surge.

I was designated by Dr. Jemison to lead the NBC delegation as the ranking officer to Ethiopia to deliver food, water, and medical supplies on behalf of the Convention. Accompanying me in the sixteen-member delegation were Reverend William J. Harvey III, secretary of the Foreign

Mission Board; Reverend Roscoe D. Cooper, editor of the NBC Voice; Ted Jemison Jr., representing his father, President Jemison; several nurses including Reverend Barbara Evans and Barbara Anderson Robinson, two physicians, and other pastors. In preparation to make the trip to help, we had to meet a protocol which required paying bribes to various Ethiopian officials, both in New York and in Addis Ababa. It was a corrupt process, but we had to gain access to those in need.

We departed JFK International Airport and arrived in the hostile political environment of Addis Ababa, Ethiopia. Part of the result of the famine conditions was the consequence of political strife by the ruling Marxist government. Upon arriving, we could feel the political tension. Our delegation was invited to the president's residence for dinner. It was noteworthy that just the month before, in the very same room, the president had his enemy killed. This atmosphere fostered fear and apprehension among our delegation.

The next day we were scheduled to go to Mekelle where the famine was most impactful. Several members of our delegation were fearful given the feeling of uncertainty around us. This sense of vulnerability was advanced by the fact that all means of communication outside of the country were cut off. Word had come to us that conflict had broken out in Mekelle, our destination. It caused some of our members to refuse to go. But after strong encouragement, we all boarded the bus to Mekelle where we set up a relief center for housing over 250,000 Ethiopians. We distributed over 2,000 pounds of wheat flour, and our doctors and nurses provided medical assistance. There was so much despair, yet the Ethiopians managed a smile of gratitude for our help.

Our next trip was not reassuring. The plane was a vintage McDonnell Douglas 1941, DC3 two-engine cargo plane. Our luggage, which included filming equipment, was handled by a person who appeared to be a porter who wore his red cap backward. When he turned his cap around, he became the pilot. On this ancient plane, we flew to Bati. We landed on a dusty airstrip that Ted Jemison called "a surreal experience," and it was. We were met by two machine-gun-mounted Jeeps that had been commandeered by the rebels who were in battle with the Marxist government that was in charge at that time. We were in the midst of a truly life-threatening experience. We began to investigate the circumstances around us. I recall seeing animals and people collapsed from the lack of food along the roadside.

After a long day at the camp in Bati, we took up shelter at a local guest house. They could not accommodate all the members of our delegation. We decided to give the accommodations to the females and elders who were traveling with us. The rest of us slept on the bus. The night was long and made us anxious by the sound of gunshots nearby. We returned to Addis Ababa and prepared to leave Ethiopia, emotionally spent, after nine days. After the threatening tensions of our visit to Ethiopia, upon landing in Frankfurt, Germany, to get our connection to the USA, I along with others kissed the ground to be safely back in a democratic nation.

Serving as general secretary in the Jemison administration gave me, as a young pastor, tremendous exposure and opportunity for growth. As secretary I had to be present at every session of the annual, midwinter, mid-year, and various regional and state meetings of the Convention. As a consequence, I heard every variety of preaching across the diverse landscape of the Black church. The exposure enriched my spirituality as well.

Moreover, I had the honor to assist in visioning, planning and supervision of the construction of the National Baptist World Center in Nashville, Tennessee, the signature accomplishment of the Convention under the Jemison Administration. It was a proud moment in the history of the National Baptist Convention. It was the first building we had built in over sixty years. Not since the building of the Sunday School Publishing house in April 1925 had we erected a new facility. The building came with the high expectations of a new era for the National Baptist Convention.

The Convention aligned with the National Association for the Advancement of Colored People (NAACP) around several critical issues. The most significant events during our tenure affecting African Americans were the 1984 and 1988 presidential campaigns of Jesse Jackson. The Convention was energized by his performance, determination, and capacity as demonstrated in his campaign. His longtime association with the pastors gave him unequaled access to the Black church. His message and profile ignited enthusiasm, positive self-esteem, and hope among Black people. More than intangible impact, the campaign delivered literal change in the political landscape of African Americans.

The political outcome of the 1984 and 1988 campaigns resulted in unprecedented numbers of Blacks being elected to office at all levels, from county commissioners, to mayors, to Congress, to the first African American governor in the United States, Virginia Governor Lawrence Douglas Wilder. This was all a result of an expanded political consciousness awakened by the Jackson Campaign.

I had the responsibility of coordinating the Convention's broad footprint in helping turn out the vote and giving Reverend Jackson exposure to our churches and state organizations. The Convention, driven by pastors at the local level, played a vital role in the '84 and '88 campaigns.

During Dr. Jemison's tenure, we were invited to the White House by three United States presidents. First, we were invited by President Ronald Reagan during our second annual session in Washington, D. C. in 1984. Mr. Reagan was gracious and charming but, in my opinion, his policies have proved to be detrimental to African Americans. We had a pleasant meeting with George H. W. Bush early in his tenure, but I cannot identify any tangible impact we made on him or he on us. This was verified later by the fact that he nominated Clarence Thomas to the Supreme Court to replace the legendary Thurgood Marshall, a nomination we opposed in collaboration with other Black national church and civil rights organizations.

Then came William Jefferson Clinton, who offered a hopeful sign to Blacks by the number of Blacks he appointed to his cabinet and to positions held by Blacks for the first time. He was affectionately referred to as "the first Black president." Mr. Clinton was accessible and friendly.

I visited the White House several times during the Clinton administration, both with Dr. Jemison and unaccompanied. Black people put a lot of trust in President Clinton. Our support was unwavering. He still remains somewhat popular among African Americans. Nevertheless, history has shown that his policies around welfare reform, prison reform, and prison expansion have had devastatingly negative consequences on Black people.

The closing months of the Jemison administration were met with some apprehension by Dr. Jemison. While he had instituted tenure at the behest of the members of the Convention, which was a reaction to the twenty-nine-year term of his predecessor, he indicated that he did not believe in a limit on how long a president could serve. Nevertheless, he acquiesced to the adoption of term limits. As he got closer to the end of his term, he regretted having supported tenure in light of the things he wanted to complete, among which was the payoff of the mortgage on the Baptist World Center, which was the signature accomplishment of his administration.

As we came to the closing years of Dr. Jemison's leadership, he delegated more and more to me as the general secretary. In September 1993, he designated me to chair the annual session of the Convention in New York City. My years of service as secretary gave me tremendous exposure to what was necessary in planning a successful event. I received incredible support and leadership from the Empire State Baptist Convention, a component of the National body. We hosted more than 60,000 delegates and gave the Convention one million dollars towards the mortgage of the World

Center. It was among the most successful convenings of the National Baptist Convention in its long history.

Over the thirteen years of my service as general secretary, I made many contacts and had garnered large support to succeed President Jemison. At the close of the 1993 session, it was acknowledged that there was not sufficient support to address tenure. Dr. Jemison then released me to run with his full blessing and endorsement.

Serving as general secretary of the National Baptist Convention was a tremendously impactful and pivotal moment in my career. It gave me occasions to develop skills that would continue to open doors and equip me with the exposure and capacity to take advantage of new opportunities. Indeed, it was an expression of God's grace towards me!

While engaged in the affairs of the secretariat of the NBC, I still had a church to pastor. By the grace of God my congregation thrived during my years as general secretary. We had steady growth, and I felt loved by their unrelenting support for all I was doing.

Remaining Grounded

WHILE ENGAGED IN THE BROADER RESPONSIBILITIES OF THE denomination as general secretary of the National Baptist Convention, I remained dually focused on my assignment as a local pastor. The duality of being a local pastor and a national religious leader has had a tremendous impact on shaping my contribution to the ministry. Experiencing ministry from the standpoint of the local parish and the person in the pew gives one sensitivity to the issues facing people in the day-to-day struggles of life. Visiting the sick, ministering to the brokenhearted, responding to the needs of youth, companioning with the elderly, and attending to the social justice challenges of community raises one's competence and compassion as a leader. Is this not what we know of the grace of the incarnation, the life, and ministry of the historical Jesus? It is at this level of serving the lives of others that we acquire Christian authenticity.

Serving as pastor of Grace, as I served the larger national community, kept me connected to the priorities of our people. The people of Grace, our lay leadership and staff, have provided unconditional love and support for me as my ministry has included expanding horizons across the years. I have been blessed by the extraordinary ministry of the chairs of our deacons ministry, which have included Ozzie Reuben, Joseph Brown, Wallace Williams, Francis Kimber, Richard Thompson, and our trustee ministry under Marjorie Dash and Hurdy Watler. These leaders poured blessings into my life as have many others who now reside in the "Silent City."

Words cannot express the impact of my partner in this ministry of nearly thirty years in that of our brilliant and dedicated Minister of Music, Derrick L. James, whose leadership has helped sustain creativity and enthusiasm in our witness. What a gift of grace he has been and continues to be. His expert presentation of the multiple genres of the great music of the Black church has been an inspiring escort to my weekly preaching assignment. I have always had a love for the soulful music of the church and his witness has enhanced it. He has fed my soul!

When I took on the responsibilities of general secretary of the Convention, Deacon Richard Thompson, who was vice-chair of the deacons ministry, made himself available to assist me. He was a retired New York City police officer. Given the demands of my new responsibility, it was a blessing to have him accompany me at the annual sessions. His expertise in providing security and coordinating the activities of my office, where as many as 60,000 delegates attended, proved to be invaluable. Far beyond his activities in assisting me with the work of the convention, he has been an extraordinary partner in the ministry and a devoted friend.

Additionally, my office was attended to by three wonderful members of Grace: Dorothy Coleman, Edna Harris and Edwina Ramsey, who volunteered from the very beginning to create a competent support team. My work as secretary was truly an extension of the ministry of Grace Baptist Church. Our congregation has met many challenges with openness and grace, which has informed my understanding, personal growth, and thinking, and which ultimately affected my national leadership.

Unfortunately, many Black churches perpetuate a legacy of female exclusion from ordained leadership in the church, reflective of the broader culture. Amazingly, Black congregations, which were and are predominantly populated by women, were citadels of sexism reinforced by poor societal influences and practices as well as selective misinterpretation of scripture. This resulted in the exclusion of women in the ordained leadership of the church. It is sadly remarkable that though clearly understanding the sin of racism, the church could not or did not recognize the sin of sexism. Even denominations composed of churches that were free to interpret the scriptures independently were dominated by a sexist view of women that was broadly and strictly sanctioned in practice and theology.

Having been oriented and ordained in the tradition of the Black Baptist church, I embraced the status quo sexist practices I inherited as a "Black Baptist pastor." It never occurred to me that the church was sexist, nor that sexism and racism were essentially the same. It is true that the oppressor never gets tired of oppressing. The oppressed have to decide they will no longer be oppressed.

I was confronted with this contradiction between the gospel we preached and the church's practice regarding the exclusion of women when a relatively new member of our congregation, Flora Wilson-Bridges, requested a meeting with me. During the meeting, she shared her call to ministry, which at first presented a dilemma for me given the fact that our church had never recognized a woman as a minister. But after listening to and reflecting on her call, my reluctance dissipated. I found in her call all of the elements of my call to ministry. Therefore, to dismiss her call as inauthentic would be to invalidate my own. That encounter opened my eyes to the glaring contradiction of the gospel that was manifest in every aspect of our church's practice.

I recommended to our congregation that she be granted ministry credentials after her initial sermon. My request was approved to my delight and surprise without any opposition. She became the first female minister in the nearly100-year history of our church. The impact of that decision was far-reaching and transformational in many future aspects of the church's life. It lifted the veil to see other ways in which women were discriminated against in the church. It awakened in other women a call to ministry that they were suppressing. Not long after that, the deacons ministry, which was composed solely of men, accepted and presented to the church my recommendation that women should be included fully and formally as a part of the diaconate of Grace Baptist Church. The decision was structurally transformational in that women would participate in the highest places of service in the church.

However, the recommendation was initially not approved by the congregation, primarily defeated by the women's leadership of the church—a result I did not anticipate.

Prior to submitting my recommendation to the congregation that women should be permitted to serve as deacons, the female leadership of the church was accommodated by being bestowed a corrupted title and position lacking impact known as deaconess. The creation was an accommodation intended to appease women. It was structural oppression. The women had bought in to it as a place of recognition. Some of those women who were deaconesses were resistant to change, while others were resistant to a new power paradigm.

Moreover, all were influenced by the misperception that the deaconess represented a position of authority. Even though Grace Baptist Church was organized by five women in 1888, women accepted a second-class status in the life of the church based on gender. We were dealing with profoundly ingrained inferiority. I took this occasion to address their misperception. I invited them to our home to candidly discuss the role of deaconess.

I concluded our discussion with this analysis. "What do you say of a person who prepares the meal, sets the table, cleans up and washes the dishes but cannot serve the meal or stand at the table when the meal is being served and is given a title of accommodation to appease a lack of authenticity? That is who you are as a deaconess at Grace Baptist Church," I said. They departed determined to make a change, which they did. At the next church meeting, we elected female deacons and eliminated the deaconess ministry.

Less than ten years later, we elected Francis Kimber our first female chair of the deacons ministry. The unforeseen benefits of a gender-inclusive deacons ministry included the change of atmosphere in the meetings of the deacons from that of the exclusive male club to a higher focus of service. It also modeled positive self-esteem for our girls. What an extension of favor to be a part of such a transforming of "herstory" in Grace Baptist Church. This experience helped me to understand the kinship between racism, which I naturally opposed at my core, and sexism.

This early episode in my ministry provided a prism through which I would view the gospel as an opponent of any form of oppression, whether it be racism, sexism, ageism, genderism, or classism. I am convinced that to be tolerant of any form of oppression is an affront to the gospel of Jesus Christ. The engagement in discrimination of any vestige of difference in human creation is a denial of grace. Whatever our differences, we all bear in our diversity the fingerprint of God. We did not participate in the selection of our diversity; our diverse traits are divine endowments.

As the years progressed, our congregation continued to flourish. Much of the exposure and opportunity I experienced while serving at a national level blessed our church as well. Our first housing project, Grace House, was a direct result of my being general secretary of the Convention. The visibility I received helped brand Grace as an example of a relevant ministry. Our success as a church was not automatic. It has required constant nurturing. Our unity has been our greatest strength.

The Mount Vernon community and metropolitan New York area provided a powerful platform to identify and address the critical issues facing the African American community collective. This grassroots access provided a window whereby I could have an authentic understanding of what was before us as a people. Those who would be our leaders must be grounded in intimate knowledge of our experience.

The other dimension of grounding for me, aside from the church, was family. Seven years after moving to New York in 1982, my mother and father moved to Mount Vernon to be near their grandchildren and us. Their move was a blessing. It provided them with access to their grandchildren, and our children benefited from their grandparents' love. Inez and I were also always covered when we needed to travel or fulfill commitments. Moreover, my parents were very active in the church. Shortly after becoming members, they were asked to join the deacons ministry. What a gift of grace to have my parents serving in the deacons ministry where I was pastor. They were powerful leaders and well-loved by the congregation. I also welcomed their counsel, and I could trust that their advice was coming from a place of unconditional love. Though I was their pastor, and they respected me in that role, at the end of the day I was their child. I was comforted by their escort through the changing terrain of my life.

I also found great solace in my children, Orchid, William III, and my stepdaughter, Katrina. Among my most pleasant surprises was William's surrender to ministry. He was determined to be anything but a preacher. He is a strong-willed person, but God finally won out! The girls were much less rebellious than William, though they provided different challenges. They are a blessing to Inez and me. Inez made our home a place of serenity and renewal for our children and me. Though there were times of storm, calm ultimately prevailed. Along the way, I have not only witnessed the grace of God in my life, but I have seen it in the lives of others. The only explanation for how one makes it through life is the grace of God functioning on their behalf.

Some encounters stand out in my mind; among them is Enid Hay, a young woman who showed up at our church broken and destitute. She had run from an abusive relationship in Detroit and ended up in Mount Vernon, not knowing anyone. A stranger told her about Grace and told her, "They will help you." When she showed up at Grace, she had no money, and her Jamaican dialect was so thick she could hardly be understood. She was separated from her children in Jamaica and had nowhere to stay. We embraced her by meeting her pressing needs, helped her find a place to stay, coached her, and employed her. Fast forward twenty years: she has earned her bachelor's and master's degrees in social work from Columbia University as a single parent, and I had the privilege of watching her march across the stage at Columbia to receive her degrees.

Her children are with her now, and she owns her home and provides foster care for an autistic child as part of our church staff. She has been executive director of Grace Community Development Corporation for more than fifteen years. I have witnessed grace in her life. There are hundreds of young people who have passed through the programs of our church, who have been victimized by marginalized school systems, by biased criminal justice forecasting their future incarceration, by exclusionary economic policy, and by abusive sociology. Yet they have all been salvaged by the grace of God. Then there are those in the pews each Sunday who bear witness to the grace of God who have endured sickness, heartache, trials, and tribulations and have found the face of God.

Some people come into your life unannounced. You have no idea how they got there, but the friendship becomes a gift of grace. Louie Difrancesco is an Italian fellow that I met on the track while jogging in Scarsdale. We could not at face value have been more different. He was a fireman, a kind of "Archie Bunker" in opinions and prejudices (his description not mine). I was a Black preacher with activist leanings. One day, after about a month of walking on the track, he asked me, "Franklyn, what do you do? What kind of work?"

"I am a preacher," I said.

"What is that?" Louie blurted.

I laughed. "I'm like a priest."

"Wow. I thought you were a drug dealer, driving a Mercedes and coming to the track in the late morning every day."

This marked the beginning of a more than thirty-year friendship that indeed has been a gift of grace. Louie's assessment of our friendship is captured in his statement, "I met Reverend as a hater, and he turned it into love."

I have had the opportunity to witness grace in the ministers that I have had occasion to mentor. I have had a front-row seat to the evolving ministries of my sons and daughters in ministry; among them are leading pastors: Reverend Dr. Flora Wilson-Bridges, Rendall Memorial Presbyterian Church, New York; Dr. Adolphus C. Lacey, Bethany Baptist Church, Brooklyn, New York; Dr. Jawanza Karriem Colvin, Olivet Institutional Baptist Church, Cleveland, Ohio; Dr. Howard John Wesley, Alfred Street Baptist Church, Alexandria, Virginia; Dr. Edward Mulraine, Unity Tabernacle Baptist Church, Mount, Vernon, New York; and my staff colleagues the Reverends William M. Mizell, Sheila Simmons, Dr. Lillian Reynolds, and many other ministers whom I have had the privilege to nurture. The witness of grace in them is a joy to me.

I watched how faith has functioned in their lives as a testimony to the grace of God. Their stories alone could provide content for another volume. Among those I have had the opportunity to witness the grace of God in their ministry is one whom I have had the most significant access to: my son William Franklyn Richardson III. His story is a testimony of favor, and his struggle with and surrender to the call of ministry for Christ is a joy to my soul.

Seventeen years ago, I received a request from a member of Grace Church, Deacon Lloris Williams-Carney, who had recently relocated to Port Saint Lucie, Florida. Each time she returned to Mount Vernon, she asked if I would be willing to come to Port Saint Lucie and start a church. At first, I just knew she was joking, but she persisted each time she came back. Subsequently, she asked to meet with me to further discuss her request. I agreed to meet, and she explained that Port Saint Lucie was a developing city with a growing African American community, and there was not a church for our community. She asked again if I would be willing to start a church at Port Saint Lucie. I responded, "If you can get fifty potential members to sign a letter inviting me, I will come and discuss the possibility of starting a church." I was sure that would end it. To my surprise, a month later, she returned with the letter signed by one hundred Port Saint Lucie residents. Committed—off I went to Port Saint Lucie.

Upon my arrival, I met with the group and listened to their concerns and desires to have a church in Port Saint Lucie for the Black community. When the conversation turned to ask me if I would come, I said, "I have never started a church, but your sincerity is contagious. I am willing to come to Florida every Wednesday, have a worship service, and begin to bond together and see what happens." I started in September 2002. Grace Church in New York adopted the church in Florida as a mission objective of our congregation. I preached regularly for four years, assisted by ministers from our New York church staff. The congregation evolved to the point that some felt we needed a resident pastor. I agreed, but I knew of no options at the time.

Subsequently, William came forward and asked if I would consider sending him to serve in Florida. He had preached there on several occasions and was willing to adjust his plans to serve. He assumed the responsibility in February 2006, and the ministry has continued to flourish under his leadership modeling the ministry of Grace in New York. Many souls have come to Christ, and the membership has greatly expanded. Not only does grace appear in the strict sense of religion but also the day to day of human encounters. These encounters have kept me and nurtured my faith. As my colleague, Senior Bishop Elizabeth Eaton of the Evangelical Lutheran Church, once said: "Grace is in every breath we take."

Divine Value

THE ENCOUNTERS OF WOMEN WITH JESUS IN THE NEW Testament are profoundly instructive and inspiring. When we hear the great stories of women who met Jesus during His earthly pilgrimage, we are powerfully inspired. I don't know that there is a more powerful encounter than the one told to us in the thirteenth chapter of Luke. There was a woman who had been ill for eighteen years—for eighteen years she could not stand straight. It was not just the disease that afflicted her; it was also the attitudes of society, her economic condition, and the mental toll everything brought upon her.

She could not work. She did not have the capacity to sustain herself, especially if she was not married. She had no value in Jewish society because in order for women to have societal value, they had to be attached to a man as a wife.

She was ruined because of societal and economic circumstances. She was afflicted because she was a woman! She was devalued in the minds of the patriarchs of the text. The entire cultural mentality at that time was one of persecution of women. But Jesus' lived theology was different. He saw her, He empowered her, and He legitimized her.

First, He saw her. It is easy to quickly read past that and miss the significance of that moment. However, Jesus saw her from far away. Jesus was teaching the men in the synagogue in the inner sanctum where only men were permitted. Through the curtain between the inner and outer sanctums, He saw her. That means she mattered to Him. One of the most demoralizing things that can happen in a society is to be ignored. She had been ignored, but He recognized her. Not only did He see her, He sought her. Today, what we need is somebody to see us. We live in a world where the color of your skin can make you invisible. Your pain and your circumstance are invisible.

If you are a woman, in many places, you have no value, you are ignored. If you are one of several minority groups, you are ignored. If you are poor, you are ignored. If you don't live in a certain neighborhood or have certain credentials, you are ignored. You have no value. I thank God that Jesus recognizes me. He knows that I am a child of God. I am somebody because He recognizes me. He sees me. He sees my pain. He sees my misery. He sees the woman afflicted for eighteen years. Because of this, He wanted to do something for her. He empathized with what she was going through. Consequently, He broke the rules. He called her from the outside to the inside and we know because, "He laid his hands on her." He broke all the rules. I can just imagine the widening of all the eyes of the men in that place. Jesus had called a woman into their "club," and He was going to heal her on the sabbath day. You know the men were beside themselves.

In that moment, He empowered her. He put his hands on her and said, "Woman be thou loose." And the text says (this is a powerful line), "She stood straight up." When she stands up, she has new self-esteem. She first received self-esteem when He called her from outside of the temple and told her to come in. Everyone saw that she mattered to Jesus then, but it wasn't until she stood straight up that her own self-esteem was repaired. When you have been down for eighteen years, you are plagued with low self-esteem and self-worth, bound by a myriad of prejudices. As a woman, and especially as a woman in her condition, she would never be seen to be worthy enough to occupy a prime seat in the outer temple. She was in the back of the room.

He empowered her and gave her the courage to stand up and be what she was made to be. That's what God does! That's what He does to the least and the last. There are people on the streets that don't matter to many people, but they matter to the Lord. There are people that many in society ignore, but they matter to the Lord. There are people that get ignored because of the color of their skin, but they matter to the Lord. There are people who are ignored because of their gender, gender identity, or sexuality, but they matter! They matter to Jesus! They matter! He sees them and wants to empower them as well.

Not only does Jesus empower the woman, but He legitimizes her as well. You can be recognized and empowered, but you can't be what you ought to be until you have been legitimized. Some people are empowered and recognized, but they are still not legitimized. They are not authentic. But Jesus legitimizes this woman. When the men see Jesus invite the woman inside and heal her, the chief synagogue leader says, "You know we have six days to do healing, and on the seventh day, we are supposed to rest because it is the sabbath. It seems that He could do His healing on those other days." Jesus said, "We are not made for the sabbath; the sabbath is made for us." The sabbath is not the rule.

Many folks in the church have so many rules that they are too paralyzed to be or do any good. We have so many formalities and so many definitions of "rightness" that we restrict people from fulfilling their potential. We are so stuck on traditions and captured by yesterday that we fail to be a value to tomorrow.

So, the men started quoting the Bible to Jesus. The devil knows the Bible, and sometimes it is hard to tell whether or not it is the devil. The devil quotes scripture all the time. Through these men, the devil started quoting scripture to Jesus. Jesus said, "Well, I tell you that you are hypocrites. You are hypocrites because you detach your oxen and your animals and take them to give them water on the sabbath. But this woman, is she not in fact a daughter of Abraham?"

When Jesus said that, those fellows in the temple thought, "Great God, I've never heard that! There has never been anything spoken in all of the Old Testament about a daughter of Abraham." The Old Testament only spoke about the sons of Abraham. But Luke says, "She is a daughter of Abraham." That means that Abraham has daughters too. Abraham is the father of the faith. What he said is, "She is valuable because she is Abraham's daughter and she has a right to fulfill her purpose and her life and her value in God." She is a daughter of Abraham. That means she has power and she is empowered! She has divine value. She has legitimacy.

If I have divine value, I really don't care what you think about me. If I have divine value, I don't care whether you care about the color of my skin. If I have divine value, I really don't care whether I'm a woman or whether I'm gay or straight. It really doesn't make any difference to me if I have value in the eyes of God. When I have value in the eyes of God, I'm legitimate! I'm somebody because God made me, and God does not make junk. He signed His name on me! From the kink in my hair, to the thickness of my lips, to the swiggle of my hips, to the melanin in my skin—He made me! I am legitimate because He made me! I am no accident or coincidence; I am the result of divine intentionality.

When He said the woman was legitimate, they were ashamed. After this story ends, I cannot believe that this was the end of this woman's journey.

We don't hear any more about her in the Bible, but I know that there is more to her story because no one can be hunched over for eighteen years, meet Jesus, gain power and legitimacy, and then go away. I don't know the rest of her story, but I know she had to be a witness for the Lord. I am sure people would see her on the street and say, "Aren't you the woman who was hunched over for eighteen years?"

And she would say, "Yes, I am the woman. I met Jesus and He turned my life around. He gave me a new walk and new talk. He gave me new value and I will never be the same."

Some sophisticated Christians might have walked up to her and said, "Why are you doing all of this?" But if they knew her story and knew what she had been through, they would understand her praise.

Since I met Jesus my life has been forever changed. The Bible doesn't tell us what happened, but you know that the temple no longer defined her. When you have Jesus in your life it's not possible to be a second-class citizen living beneath your potential. When Jesus is in your life, every place is your place, mountains and valleys are your place! Jesus knows who you are. He knows your name and He has called you to be empowered.

CHAPTER TEN

Losing to Win

As we came to the close of Dr. Jemison's tenure as president of the National Baptist Convention, I once again felt an ambition to one day be president of the National Baptist Convention. I considered my early selection as general secretary to be an indication that becoming president could happen. I served loyally, every day, as an occasion to prepare myself for what I perceived to be God's will. My ambition never obstructed my loyalty to President Jemison. As time went on, he counseled me on the skills vital to become an effective leader of the National Convention. I was approached early on by pastors and lay leaders with the prospect of becoming the next president. I found their comments to be self-affirming as they were in line with my desire. Nevertheless, I spent a season in prayer searching to know the mind of God on whether I should seek the presidency.

As in all things, we hear God's response through the Spirit and act in faith to what we have understood Him to say. I solicited God to let me know His will regarding my desire to serve as president. As best I could discern, at that time, God said run.

I would not launch a campaign until Dr. Jemison decided what he was going to do regarding his future. With one year left in his term, at the close of our annual session in New York City in 1993, he told me that he was not going to challenge tenure and that he felt that I was prepared to become president. He released me to launch my campaign. My team was waiting and ready. We began the journey to New Orleans, where the election would take place the following year. This, in itself, was a good thing for me, given that Dr. Jemison was also president of the Louisiana Baptist Convention with considerable influence over the state. It was also helpful that I had spent so much time in Louisiana during my tenure as secretary.

It was conventional wisdom that my chances of victory in my bid to become national president would be enhanced by winning the presidency at the state level. Therefore, my first hurdle would be to get elected president in my home state of New York. It was something I felt I could accomplish given the years of service and privilege I had given to New York as national secretary. The election would take place in Buffalo, New York. The October after the National Annual Session, the state convention was convened, and my name was presented by the nominating committee as their choice to be president.

However, the Reverend Samuel Austin, Pastor of Brown Memorial Baptist Church in Brooklyn, New York and a native son of Buffalo, was also a candidate. He had not gotten the nomination from the committee but contested and had his name put in consideration. The procedure delayed the process, causing a busload of my supporters from Long Island to leave early in order to catch their plane. We lost the election by two votes. Needless to say, I was extremely disappointed at the outcome, even though I had the overwhelming support of the pastors of New York. There is something discouraging about failure, no matter how it can be explained.

Reverend Austin was my immediate predecessor at Grace Baptist Church in Mount Vernon. There may have been some remaining negative residue between us, or his own negotiated interest, that caused him to support my national opponent, the Reverend Henry James Lyons. Looking back, it might be said that I lost the national election that night in Buffalo.

After assessing the fallout of that disappointment, our team felt we should push forward and could still prevail at the national election. We moved full steam ahead and began organizing, identifying support, raising funds, and scheduling rallies and appearances. The campaign journey was long and arduous. I was assisted in my pursuit by the dedicated efforts of my campaign manager, the Reverend Boise Kimber of First Calvary Baptist Church of New Haven, Connecticut, who proved to be a devoted friend and confidant throughout the years. We mapped out a plan that identified the cities, state conventions, and conferences I would need to visit. We organized a national campaign committee composed of supporting pastors from across the country. We received tremendous support from New York and across the country.

A critical occurrence in the campaign was when the Reverend David Mathews, president of the largest state convention in Mississippi, agreed to be my running mate as vice president at large. Dr. Mathews had been a loyal fixture in the Convention serving as regional vice president in both the J. H. Jackson and T. J. Jemison administrations. He represented our effort in the older generation and the critical South. His engagement in the campaign was aggressive and coordinated.

I traveled endlessly across the country delivering my campaign message. I was scheduled for several events every week. Sometimes I was accompanied by a delegation of supporters and other times I was alone. It was physically grueling, but I did not relent. I felt that we had an opportunity to contribute to progressive change for Black people. I was not running simply to be a denominational leader but to make the Convention transformational in the lives of African Americans.

We were the largest Black organization in America. We represented upwards of 25,000 congregations with more than ten million members. We were potentially a political, economic, and social force because we spoke to our constituents each week. I was convinced, given our progressive vision and the capacity to implement strategies, that we could leverage our strength to change our circumstance for the good. Black people then and now are at the bottom of every indicator for quality of life. I was certain that our convention had the capacity to lead that change.

It was this vision that got me up each day. The task of our campaign was to communicate our vision so that it could be acceptable to an organization that was considered biblically conservative. Many in the Convention believed that the church's only value was to get us to heaven. They didn't believe that the church could and should transform the hell our people were living in every day. To quote a familiar statement, "We are so heavenly focused that we are no earthly good." Far too many have a singular view of faith that believes religion is only to get us through a dismal context and fail to see that it is also intended to change the dismal context. My campaign sought to convey this notion.

If we remained disengaged, not addressing the issues congregations were dealing with, we would become irrelevant and the denomination would die. We had to become a servant organization to survive. The Convention had to enable pastors to answer satisfactorily the fundamental question asked by my members in the pew: "Pastor, why are we members of the National Baptist Convention?" Our inability to answer that question continues to haunt us.

One of the most disquieting conversations I had during the campaign was with the late Reverend Manuel Scott Sr., pastor of the Saint John Baptist Church, Dallas, Texas. I loved Dr. Scott. He had been a mentor to me since the beginning of my ministry. He was a model preacher. He is singularly responsible for me abandoning the use of a manuscript or notes while preaching. He had always been one of the most reliable encouragers in my career.

I approached him about supporting my candidacy for president and he said, "Rich, they are not going to elect you president of this Convention. You are too progressive for this group. The Lord has some far greater things for you to do!"

I am sure he felt he was speaking to me in my best interest, but I was not expecting that. I was extremely disappointed in his assessment. I did not want to hear his truth. However, like Mary upon receiving the message from the angel, "I hid in my heart" what he said while I went forward with the demands of my campaign.

While contemplating this project I shared with Dr. Riggins Earl, one of the ministers that supported my candidacy and currently a theological educator, that I was writing my memoir, which would include my NBC years. Immediately he suggested that I do not leave out the theological, political, and cultural environment of the time. He wrote me this letter:

> *Brotherman, I am so delighted to see you*
> *bring to light your own reflections on what*
> *happened during your run for president*
> *of the National Baptist Convention. Your*
> *citation of the words of Dr. Scott about*
> *"your youth and progressive ideas" obviously*
> *gets to the heart of the problem that you were*
> *facing. Here are some hypothetical questions*
> *for what they are worth. Had this convention*
> *ever had a president as young and progressive*
> *minded as you were as a candidate for the*
> *presidency? Was it an unwritten law, or*

a social custom, in the convention to reject
young and progressive minded leadership? It
seems to me that this is why the convention
politically saw the need to support tenure as
a divine mandate. Is it the case that whatever
changes that took place under Jemison
happened because he was an old man and
perceived as lesser of a threat to the Jackson
regime and ideology? Would Jemison have
been elected to succeed Jackson had he been
your age at the time that he ran in Miami?

Reading through writings and listening to the
sermons of Dr. Jackson clearly shows that
he was a hardcore conservative, theologically
and politically. The convention had adopted
the mind of J.H. Jackson. Oral tradition,
among older Black preachers, report that
Lyons and Shaw were disciples of Jackson.
Your running for office symbolized the
coming of age of a generation of young
preachers and pastors who had been
theologically, intellectually, emotionally and
socially influenced by Martin Luther King,
Jr. The "clarion call" for social change in
America came from Martin King and not
Jackson. The latter called for change via
individual conversion which was celebrated
in our slave heritage. Your supporting cast,
particularly of my generation of then
young preachers, for the presidency of the

convention understood the necessity of social change. You, and those of us who supported you, were perceived by the traditional elders as attackers of Jackson's ghost. The vote to remove Jackson in Miami might not have been to change the agenda of the convention, as much as it was to send papa Jackson into exile for protection. It is what we see especially in traditional African societies. Why was Dr. Jem not perceived that way? I think that it was because they still heard Jackson in Jemison's voice and saw him in Jemison's age category. In the youthful Richardson, they saw a radically erudite young leader who would possibly take the convention away from the old guard.

In hindsight brotherman, what could you have done to change the organization as its president? I know you have thought about that question. Dr. Taylor's words of consolation in his call to you that painful night in Tampa, in hindsight, sounds like the voice of God's grace and wisdom. Your vision of ministry is bigger than a dying body of reactionary Black preachers.

Rich, I hope this publication will be but the genesis of your writings on the subject. Having taught in seminary for most of my life, I am appalled that we have few, if any books, by social activist Black

preachers. Please get a scholar, given your
busy schedule, to help you produce, at a
later time, a more in depth writing of
what you are doing for future generations.

Thank you, friend, for asking me to become a
conversation partner with you on this project.

Bless your preaching and teaching bones!

Riggins

My primary opponent was the Reverend Dr. William James Shaw, Pastor of White Rock Baptist, Philadelphia, Pennsylvania. I knew Dr. Shaw from the beginning days of my ministry in Philadelphia. He was a friend of my pastor, and when I was at my home church conducting revivals, he came by on more than one occasion. I was both encouraged and intimidated by his attendance. He was a celebrated pastor, and I was a tenderfoot. He was gracious. I ran vigorously for the office, but I held him in high regard.

The Reverend Henry James Lyons was my other opponent and also pastor of Bethel Metropolitan Baptist Church in Saint Petersburg, Florida. I met him after he was appointed to regional vice president during the Jemison Administration, and he had travelled alongside me in the delegation of religious leaders to Taiwan representing the Convention in 1983.

As we got closer to the election, campaign activities heated up, requiring a greater investment of time and financial commitment by all. We succeeded in energizing our base and meeting our fundraising goals. We arrived in New Orleans on Monday, before the election, which was to be held on that Thursday, well equipped to execute our plan. We were met by a large and lively group of Louisiana pastors who made a display of the support we had in the state in an attempt to sway undecided delegates. We had made a huge investment in the outcome of the election. All indicators suggested that we were in line to be victorious. Moreover, I had remained prayerful and felt spiritually sanctioned to pursue the presidency of the Convention.

During this time I had built a relationship with President William Jefferson Clinton, and as we were approaching the election of the Convention presidency, I shared with him that I was running for president of the Convention and asked the president if he would come to the convention and speak the morning after the election in New Orleans. He agreed to come.

I continued to campaign throughout the week. The day before the election, the voting machines were put in place in the Convention Center. It would be the first time we used electronic balloting. All camps felt the process was reliable.

On the day of voting, more than 10,000 delegates voted. The night before I had been informed by members of our team that irregular activities by the Lyons campaign were taking place where the voting machines were stored. I did not put as much importance on the report as I should have, given our perception of how strong we were. If the election were delayed or cancelled, the chaos that would follow would have been unimaginable. We prayed that the outcome would not be affected by whatever shenanigans had taken place.

After a grueling and exhausting campaign, the next day ten thousand delegates gathered in the New Orleans Convention Center to elect the next president of the ten million-member National Baptist Convention. The entire day was spent by delegates from across the United States and the Bahamas casting their ballots. There were several candidates, some more probable to be elected than others. When the results were announced that evening at 10:00 PM, the Reverend Henry J. Lyons had won by an extremely thin margin. I had come in second and the Reverend Dr. William Shaw had come in third.

There was shock across the room. Reverend Lyons was considered by most unlikely to win. There was broad disbelief among the delegates and my supporters, who were visibly despaired. Significant suspicion arose immediately around the outcome of the election. The report of his supporters corrupting the computers was widely circulated and subsequently verified some time later by some who had actually participated in the scheme to rig the outcome of the election. Ultimately unrelated but related, less than two years into his tenure, Reverend Lyons was charged with stealing and corruption in the execution of his administration. He was sentenced and served four years in federal prison.

Friday morning, after the election, President Clinton came as he promised. While standing in the convention center waiting for President Clinton, tears began to run down my cheek as I wondered what God was doing. I greeted the

President at the rear entrance of the Convention Center. When he saw me, he said, "Franklyn, what happened?"

Heavy laden with disappointment I replied, "I lost in a questionable process."

"I am so sorry," he said, "I came here for you!"

I replied, "I am grateful!"

We proceeded to the Plenary Hall where he was to speak to the convention. As I sat on the stage that morning, I asked myself, "Why is this happening?" I had prayed to God and thought He had given me the go-ahead. I sat there watching my family, members of my church, and my supporters from across the country. I was bewildered. I felt grave disappointment, betrayal, defeat, and shame. I was at a dark place. But in the midst of my despair, God's grace was at work. Often in our crisis God is working on our behalf. It was in the face of failure that I truly came to realize that the presence of grace had been a constant escort on my journey and that the days ahead would not be any different.

What was born afresh in me as a result of this devastating experience was what may be called "Grace Consciousness." What a powerful and redemptive discovery. The collateral consequence of apparent failure may very well be that it sets us up to know the grace of God more completely. This experience birthed in me a perpetual acknowledgement of God's grace, evident in every step I take. As a result, I have come to see life through a prism of His favor. To trust His word that "all things work together for good to them that love God." ·

I shall never forget a "Grace Call" I received that night after the ballots had been tallied and the results announced. A sage of the pulpit and a highly celebrated pastor, the late Reverend Dr. Gardner C. Taylor, esteemed Pastor of Concord Church of Brooklyn, New York, called my suite. The gloom of despair and crushed expectations filled the room like a cloud when Inez told me I had a phone call. Dr. Taylor, with his majestic voice and relaxed rhythm, said to me, "Franklyn, I called to assure you that there is life beyond the National Baptist Convention. Lift up your head; you have joined the ranks of those who have similarly been rejected by the Convention. Yet, they have found meaning and opportunity after their rejection as I have, as did Martin Luther King Jr., and as will you. God will not abandon you. Bless you, my son. Goodnight." Those words spoken to me by this icon of the Christian church still live in my heart! The wounds of defeat cannot silence them. They yet nurture my capacity to wait on God. I am assured that God has alternate pathways for our fulfillment.

The National Baptist Convention collectively, with some few silent exceptions, under the last twenty-three years of the Jackson presidency, though it was the largest Black organization in the United States during that time, accepted the status quo. It attempted to accommodate its low self-esteem by becoming a mirror image of the oppressor's religion, the Southern Baptist Convention, in an effort to gain legitimacy, even embraced a White Jesus. This was clearly evidenced by a blond, blue-eyed Jesus hung in many Black churches across the country. In 1975, when I first became Pastor of Grace, White European angels presided over the pulpits with harps in their hands. It took some degree of political finesse to take them down.

The Black church of that era, not far removed from now, held White Western Christianity as the quintessential expression of God. These attitudes were fostered by the absence of a socially conscious denomination which gave no voice of resistance to the flourishing inferiority definition of the Negro. The Convention's critical absence and muted voice took place under the ultra-conservative leadership of Dr. J. H. Jackson for twenty-nine years.

Beyond the political disputes regarding tenure of the office of president, there was a palatable tension between those who were resistant to the denomination's non-engagement in the fight for equality and those who were content with the status quo. These two issues led to the split of the convention and the formation of the "Progressive National Baptist Convention" in 1961.

In 1982, I entered into the dynamics of convention leadership dominated by an old guard steeped in social non-engagement. I came under the leadership of Dr. Jemison who had impeccable social justice credentials. Yet there was an undying allegiance to this disengaged pietistical evangelical form of Christianity.

In some ways our historical theological allegiances and organizational affiliations had made our convention co-conspirators to our own oppression. This posture deprived our convention from being a social justice conduit for our people. When any organization fails to serve its constituency, it begins its demise.

Even to this day we have not fully overcome the collateral damage of an unaccountable and non-engaging theology, which in some way in this current season, is driving the convention to irrelevance, and unless we change, will lead our convention to extinction. Simply gathering to meet is not an indication of relevance but rather is a positive impact on those we serve.

The pull on me to lead our denomination into a progressive era was so strong that I endured two additional attempts at the presidency, in 1999 and 2004, before surrendering that God's purpose had been fulfilled in my efforts. In each election the outcomes were close and the process questionable. Each time I gained new insight and moved closer to God. Throughout the years I never felt outside of His purpose; I walked forward in faith trusting Him for my future. Sometimes it is in losing that we win! I have lost sometimes, and I have won a lot, but I have never been defeated.

We Are Not Saved

WE ARE HAUNTED BY THE NOTION THAT, LIKE IN THE ANCIENT biblical text of the prophet Jeremiah, many opportunities for reconciliation and restoration have come and gone and we, as the sons and daughters of the oppressed, are not saved. The role of the church in social justice as a ministry has always intrigued me. I suppose growing up as a Black boy, I became aware of the subtle signals of racism in American society. It seems to me that I was always unsettled about celebrating the Fourth of July. There always seemed to be an ambivalence attached to it. I instinctively felt not fully included in its patriotism.

As I grew up, I began to uncover reasons for my lack of embrace of American patriotism, beginning with my first encounters with covert racism in the South and continuing into adolescence and beyond. I grew up in the late fifties and sixties, a time of intense social unrest around the issues of racial oppression. It was the modern African American Civil Rights Era, which I define from *Brown v. Board of Education* to the death of Dr. Martin Luther King, Jr.

During this season, there was much public discourse and protest regarding the rights of Black people in the United States. During the height of the movement's intensity, I was a student in secondary school in Philadelphia, and the vibrations of what was happening in our country regarding the place of Black people could be felt by us as teenagers.

In 1963 when Dr. King gave his famous speech at the March on Washington, I watched it on television. It was an undeclared holiday in Black communities across America. I never got to meet Dr. King, though I would be shaped by his legacy. Because he was such a powerful voice and presence for the oppressed and a Black Baptist preacher, he set an expectation for Black churches and modeled behavior for a preacher. It was during this season that I refocused my career ambition to be a preacher. He modeled a relevance for the church I had not previously experienced.

This seed of social consciousness was further cultivated in me when I was a student at Virginia Union University. The ministry of the Black church had begun to view its mission through the lens of the struggle for civil rights. There was an emerging social gospel cannon for Black Christians as exemplified in the writing of Black theologians like James Hal Cone, Gayraud Stephen Wilmore Jr., and others that gave the struggle against racism a theological base. It was this social gospel which most informed my understanding of the mandates of ministry and instructed my behavior as a pastor. I have some remorse regarding this. It appears to me that those who are entering ministry today have a diminishing interest and/or understanding of the social justice mandates of the gospel, thereby leaving many of our people voiceless, helpless, ill-informed, and leaving the church with wasted opportunity. Without a commitment to social justice, how does the church offer Christocentric relevance?

The issues of social justice are intertwined with the mandates of the gospel of Jesus Christ. Those churches and Christians who are silent in their preaching and actions on social justice corrupt the gospel. The ministry and message of the historical Jesus focused on the transformation of the society. How can we do less as *His* disciples? The conditions facing the masses of Black people today are seriously unchanged from what they were in 1972. The African American community today faces a harsh reality made more threatening by the diminishing arsenal and commitment of the Black church. I have been blessed by my association with what I view as social justice extensions of my ministry, partners in the struggle for full citizenship and equality.

One of these partners is the National Urban League, which has remained stable in the fight for economic justice. It was one of the convening organizations of the 1963 March on Washington under the leadership of the late Whitney Young. I served on the board of the National Urban League for twelve years during the executive leadership tenures of John Jacobs and Hugh Price. The Urban League continues to make a vital contribution to the upward mobility of African Americans under the stellar leadership of Marc Morial.

I also, like most African Americans, feel deeply indebted for the long struggle and accomplishments of the National Association for the Advancement of Colored People (NAACP) on behalf of African Americans. During all of the twentieth century, it was defender, advocate, and voice for the aspirations of Black people. It laid the legacy of those who have paved the way and opened the doors to the opportunities we have today and continues to inspire us. The memory of such social justice legends like Thurgood Marshall, Walter White, and Oliver Hill still inspires pride in us.

I have had the privilege to share in the struggle for freedom with such exceptional leaders of the NAACP as Benjamin Hooks, who was a Black Baptist pastor and a bold voice on behalf of African Americans. In recent years I have known the partnership of Roslyn Brock, former chair of the NAACP. She is a colleague in ministry and friend in the fight for justice for our people. Hazel Dukes, an enduring witness of justice as a member of the national board and New York State Chapter president, has been a personal advocate and encourager to me and Inez. I am a life member of the NAACP and have been inspired by many who have held up the banner of the NAACP. To them all I owe a great debt.

My greatest engagement into the fight for freedom and justice has come as a result of the National Action Network (NAN). I have been a member of the board for more than twenty years. I came to NAN through the mentoring invitation and recommendation of the late Reverend Dr. Wyatt Tee Walker, senior pastor of the Canaan Baptist Church of Christ in Harlem and former chief of staff to the Reverend Dr. Martin Luther King Jr. Dr. Walker was not only my friend but mentor in the field of social justice. He often rehearsed his experiences from SCLC and immersed me in the historic encounters of the civil rights movement, its marches, the confrontations with Sheriff Bull Connors, and his time with Dr. King in the Birmingham jail. He shared the strategies they employed when planning marches and the training vital to a nonviolent protest.

I remember being hungry for every word about his historic and eyewitness accounts of the apex of our civil rights history. It was as though I was there as he unfolded the nuances of those critical experiences. Dr. Walker was an unusually gifted, well-disciplined, innovative, multi-focused, and multi-talented scholar with diverse interest. He was an author, a photojournalist, a world traveler, and a creative preacher. One of my great remembrances of our relationship was when as a member of the World Council of Churches' Central Committee, I advocated for him to be appointed a member of WCC International Commission on racism. When I returned from Switzerland after attending a Central Committee meeting, where Dr. Walker had been, unknown to him, he had been appointed. I shared the appointment with my mentor, and to see the delight on his face that day gave me special joy!

Dr. Walker was then chairman of the Board of NAN. It was interesting to see how he and Reverend Al Sharpton counter-balanced each other. They had what may be called a creative tension. It was the birth of a new vision in tension with a faithful custodian of preserving the past. The mild clashing of two generations. Upon Dr. Walker's retirement in 2006 as chairman of the board, in consultation with Reverend Sharpton, he recommended to the board that

I would succeed him as chairman. It was unanimously accepted, and I was elected. What has intrigued me, then and now, about NAN was and is its commitment to the social justice motif of Dr. King as an extension of the Black Church's legacy of liberation. The National Action Network evolved from King's teaching on non-violent social change. This was a concept introduced by Mahatma Gandhi in India, embraced by Black Christians in America and is the method at the core of the Civil Rights Movement. NAN seeks to engage the Black church and the broader African American community in continuous participation.

My alignment with the National Action Network provided me with the opportunity to participate in injustice protests that ended with me being put in jail. It was and is a badge of honor. My first encounter that ended in being jailed was outside the South African Embassy with Dr. Wyatt Tee Walker, who was also jailed for protesting apartheid in South Africa. This led to our names being placed on a banned list that made it impossible for us to go back into South Africa.

I remember, years after being jailed at the embassy, that it was announced that Nelson Mandela was going to be freed after twenty years in jail. I was faced with a dilemma. An invitation was extended to me by the African Council of Churches to come and greet Mr. Mandela as he left jail. It came at the same time I was to preach at the installation of the Reverend Prathia Hall Wynn, the first African American dean at United Theological Seminary (UTS). My dilemma was whether I should keep my commitment in Dayton or go to the historic release of Mandela from jail at Robbins Island.

Word had come to me from the media that several pastors planned to protest against my coming to Dayton as the general secretary to recognize a woman preacher being exalted to dean of the seminary. Those pastors in Dayton solved my dilemma. I recall that I said, "I reject any consideration to go to South Africa to greet Mandela as I realize that the same systemic evil and racism, which had captured Mandela, was attempting to block Dr. Wynn from being installed as the first ordained woman dean." That evil is sexism. Racism and sexism are siblings, and this is why the Lord led me to go to Dayton, Ohio. He needed me to speak to the same systemic evil that was parading itself as racism in South Africa and was parading itself as sexism in Dayton. I pray that we in the Black community will come to understand that sexism is the identical twin of racism. We must reject the many faces of the same demon.

Then there was the shooting of Amadou Diallo, 19 times, by New York police officers. Dr. Walker, Reverend Sharpton, and I were first to be arrested for protesting, followed by hundreds of citizens from New York and across the nation, including pastors, political leaders, celebrities, and ordinary citizens for over 30 days.

On many occasions I marched with Reverend Sharpton and others in protest of injustices across the South, Midwest, North, and East. I remember, very vividly, the times we marched in commemoration of the 1963 March on Washington, where Dr. King gave his "I have a dream" speech, as well as the many other times we were jailed for the cause of freedom. The protests were marked by Reverend Sharpton's signature phrase, "NO JUSTICE, NO PEACE," which has become the civil rights movement cry of this generation. The message behind the phrase is prophetic. It means that there cannot be peace in America until the inequities in the distribution of justice to people of color have been corrected. I shall long remember the feeling of value I felt when standing against injustice.

I have been delighted to partner with my friend and colleague the Reverend Al Sharpton in this great and growing enterprise. I am overjoyed to be a part of this expanding witness, as we have been encouraged by viewing the footprint of this network expand to more than one hundred chapters and five corporate offices across the country. NAN is the brainchild of the Reverend Al Sharpton, and his fierce determination is singularly responsible for what it is today. I have been blessed to stand with him.

Moreover, I have had a front row seat to the most amazing evolution of an individual I have seen in my life. To see Reverend Sharpton's rise from the streets of Bensonhurst to the suites of corporate America, to the multiple platforms of national media, and to the confidences of the president of the United States in Barack Obama, and remain consistent to his principles, is remarkable. The cataloging of his contribution in the lives of others will reveal a legacy of greatness. The work and witness of NAN has provided opportunity for our continuing participation in the legacy of liberation begun when the first Africans gave their lives resisting enslavement. Their blood has fueled future generations of protest. NAN has been a voice of protest for the many who have had no voice against the crushing forces of systemic racism. They have found encouragement and compassion because of the National Action Network.

One cannot talk about social justice without mentioning the continuing engagement and contributions of the Reverend Jesse Louis Jackson. Reverend Jackson and I became acquainted in the early years of my ministry when he came to speak at my installation banquet as pastor of Grace Church. We have continued a friendship across the changing social topography of the last forty-five years. Jesse's engagement has been transformational in the struggle for civil rights; many doors were initially opened by him through which many others have walked.

The legacy of women and men who have engaged in the battle for racial justice is long. The named and the nameless are those on whose shoulders we stand, from that first protesting African who boarded a slave ship, to the innocent incarcerated in the prisons of a failing oppressive criminal justice system today, to those who have been the victims of police brutality in our communities across the landscape of this country. To be included in the continually evolving movement for the elimination of injustice in this moment in history is to be "A Witness to Grace."

...And We Are Not Saved

It is an irrefutable fact that without the engagement of the Black church and its faith in God, the Black community would not have survived the cruelty of the past 400 years. However, this is not merely a time to focus on where we have come from or what we have been through. Our fight for freedom is not yesterday's fight but a fight that continues today. Our history must not merely be a shrine to the past but, rather, a pathway to the future.

I am sorry, however, to report that racism is alive and well. It is not in intensive care. It does not have a cold. It is not even sick. As a matter of fact, it has never been healthier in modern times than it is today. The conscience of America has gone to sleep.

The continuing remarks and actions of President Donald Trump are clear evidence of a dominant hate discourse that has captured our nation. However, do not be fooled by his misogynist, narcissistic, racist, and deplorable commentary. It is not his view alone. It represents at least thirty percent of the American population for whom he speaks!

I want to make a metaphorical application of a literal crisis referred to and assessed by the prophet Jeremiah when he described the sad state of Israel at a time of economic and social crisis. What he describes as their situation is found in the eighth chapter of Jeremiah: *"The harvest has passed. The summer has ended. And we are not saved. For the hurt of the daughters of my people, I am hurt. I am black; astonishment has taken hold of me. Is there no balm in Gilead? Is there no physician there?"*

Jeremiah describes an awful state of affairs. Israel has watched the spring harvest yield no fruit, and the summer harvest has proven to be unproductive, and they face the winter with no resources. The situation is compounded by the certainty of famine, not unlike the reality that Blacks are subjected to in this country today. America is experiencing the greatest harvest of wealth in the history of the world, but in every measurement of the quality of life, Blacks are at the bottom.

As slaves, we worked for free. Economically, we are still the last hired and the first fired. The economic comparison of Blacks to Whites has not changed much since 1971. Blacks earn considerably less when compared to their White counterparts in every category. While Black unemployment has decreased, the amount of wages among Black people are still inadequate to meet the needs of housing, health care, and food. We are not afraid to work, and more often than not, we are paid inadequately, and Black people and Black-owned businesses continue to be disproportionately affected by downturns in the economy. Black children are among the greatest victims of poverty in the United States. Many go to bed at night hungry and awaken in the morning with no relief for their hunger awaiting them.

The criminal justice system is biased against Black people, especially Black men, unable to get sufficient legal representation or navigate the judicial system, resulting in Black and Brown prison populations that are quadruple the general population. It's true: we don't do all the crime, but we do most of the time.

Jeremiah's assessment is an accurate assessment of African Americans in our nation. "The harvest is past, and the summer has ended, and we are not saved." Like Israel we have planted but have received no harvest. When one plants, one ought to expect a harvest. It is the law of nature; if you plant you should reap a harvest.

We have planted! The position that American capitalism holds over the rest of the world was possible because of slave labor. Without slave labor, the cotton gin would have been a total failure and the American economy would have collapsed. We have planted! Our forefathers built the great structures of this nation, including the United States Capitol Building, the White House, and structures all across this nation in the north, south, east, and west.

We have planted! The first person killed in the Boston Massacre and thus the first American killed in the American Revolutionary War of 1776 was Crispus Attucks—a Black man. Blacks enlisted in the Union Army, fought, and gave their lives in the Civil War of the 1860s with the expectation that victory would mean emancipation. Emancipation came but not with true freedom. Blacks fought and gave their lives in World Wars I and II, fighting for liberties for those who lived in foreign countries that they could not enjoy at home in the United States. We fought and died in the Korean War, Vietnam, the Persian Gulf, Iraq, and Iran.

When you have planted, it is reasonable to expect a harvest. It is the law of nature that when you plant you should receive a harvest. While Black people have sown seeds in the field of American development, we have not reaped a social or economic harvest. America had a harvest, but those who reaped the harvest kept it all for themselves. They not only gave it to their sons and daughters, they kept it in their families for generations. "Old money is our money."

Jeremiah, upon assessing the depth of their despair, declares, "I hurt for the hurt of my people. Astonishment has taken hold of me." This ancient preacher feels the hurt of his people. Every pastor, every church, upon assessing the state of Black people today, ought to feel deep despair for the situation of African American people.

In his despair, Jeremiah raises a poignant question, "Is there no balm in Gilead? Is there no physician there?" Gilead was the medical center of ancient Israel. Today, there is a balm; we are the balm. We can no longer depend on the good will of others to save us. Civil rights guilt is gone. Many Americans feel we have gotten all we should get. Nobody is going to save us but us. We are our own healing. We are the sons and daughters of the brave survivors of slavery, lynching, and discrimination. We are the strong ones. We must go out and leverage our resources like Moses at the Red Sea with his rod in his hand parting the waters. We must use what we have in our hands to overcome our oppression.

We must go out and vote no matter the election. If it is for dog catcher, we must be at the polls. We must go out each November and cast our vote, a vote made sacred by sacrifice and suffering of our forebears.

We must address the social ills which cause us to kill one another, destroy our own neighborhoods, disrespect our women, and celebrate derogatory descriptions of ourselves. We are the balm. We have to stop giving our money to corporations that don't act in our best interests—that do not hire us nor respect us. We must make a good education a priority for our children.

We have to speak out against injustice wherever we find it. We must resolve to stay engaged in the fight against those who suggest that we go back to Africa or Haiti. Our declaration is we will not go back until the Irish go back to Ireland. We will not go back until the British go back to Great Britain. We will not go back until the French go back France. We will not go back until the Germans go back to Germany, and then we are still not going back. This is our home!

We are the balm! We know the physician! We know the one who can heal the land. We know His name. His name is Lily of the Valley—Jesus is His name—a doctor that never lost a patient. We as Black people have only survived because of our faith in God. We know His name.

There is a balm in Gilead to heal a sin-sick soul. There is a balm in Gilead to make the wounded whole. Yes, there is a balm in Gilead! Sometimes I feel discouraged and think that my work is in vain but then the Holy Spirit revives my soul again. Yes, there is a balm in Gilead.

CHAPTER TWELVE

How Do You Say Thanks?

HOW DO YOU SAY THANKS FOR ALL THE MULTIPLE INFLUENCES that have impacted your life for good? For the people, institutions, and experiences that have shaped your perspective and inspired your aspirations? For me there are a litany of deserving entities, but here I will showcase two angels of grace.

I suppose it would be helpful to explain *why* I must say thanks. It begins with the fact that I had nothing to give when I first encountered Virginia Union University. I was only in a posture to receive. When VUU finished pouring into me, my situation completely changed; I could then pour into it. My gratitude is born of an awareness of the gifts of opportunity VUU gave to me. After the gift of a college education given me by VUU, I found my life not only empowered by the completion of that educational opportunity, but also by my association with the institution. I was given considerations simply because I was a student at VUU. It started when I was a freshman. Assisted by the faculty, I was placed in remediation to overcome my reading deficiencies. The fact that I received a call at the undergraduate school to preach at my first pastorate is a consideration granted to me because I was a student, not a graduate, at VUU. Who knows how differently my future would have been altered if it were not for the opportunities extended to me by VUU? My association with Union is foundational in my life and the achievements I have accomplished.

The challenge that faces many HBCUs is that many alumni fail to express their gratitude in a tangible way. No matter what we paid for tuition, it only represents a partial portion of the cost of our education. In many cases our institutions were birthed by people who had extremely limited resources and most of whom had no college education themselves. Our forebears put nickels, dimes, and quarters together to make these citadels of hope possible. They built these colleges and universities in the sacred expectation that there would come a generation who would benefit from their sacrifice.

The good news is that we, the next generation, have arrived and benefited from the investment of our forebears. Unfortunately, we for the most part have not made the survival of HBCUs a priority. It is said that their nickels built HBCUs, and we, with our thousands, cannot sustain them. It is not my intention to overstate the lack of support by HBCUs' alumni, but to heighten the expectation of our reinvestment in our institutions. Some of us don't give because we have allowed the larger issue of the mission of these institutions to be obstructed by some individual conflict where someone who worked for the school mistreated us. We are graduated now, with a job, and still holding that incident as justification for our not supporting the school.

Secondly, some of us have fallen for the lie that HBCUs are no longer necessary, now that we can go to predominately White institutions (PWIs) and get a better education. However, the statistics do not bear that notion to be true. PWIs accept more African Americans and graduate less than do historically Black institutions. In addition, HBCUs reinforce confidence in students whose educational potential has been sabotaged by inferior public schools in Black communities as a result of the underfunding of public education, especially in those communities.

Thirdly, our institutions have not made it clear to our students, while they are matriculating, that there is an expectation that when they have graduated, they will pay it forward. Too many of us think that once I have graduated and paid my tuition, I have finished my obligation. This attitude disempowers our institutions' growth and capacity to serve the needs of the Black community.

The question becomes for many HBCU alumni not only "How will I say thanks?" but more fundamentally, "Will I say thanks?" I am fortunate to have seized the opportunity to say thanks to Virginia Union University not only with my resources but with my time and influence. It is a sense of profound grace that prompts my gratitude. I cannot express how fulfilled I am in turning back to the institutions which gave me so much, when no one else would. This ought to birth in us exuberance to give back to these institutions.

The historic Black college is one of two surviving institutions of the African American community; the other is the Black church. Most of our private HBCUs were born in the heart of the Black church. This partnership between the Black church and the Black college has propelled untold numbers of Black people forward into the future. Yet many of these Black colleges are struggling to avoid closure. We must do all we can to save both. Most historic Black private colleges that have avoided closure are struggling. The reality is that we as a people need these colleges now as much as ever. I have had the opportunity to look at the challenges facing a private historic Black university from the inside out as a member of the trustee board of Virginia Union University. The private HBCU is the most threatened of historically Black colleges in that they are not eligible in most states to receive state funding.

The past several years as a trustee has raised my understanding of how these colleges function. As a result of my serving in this capacity, I have a postgraduate awareness regarding the challenges these institutions face. Our administrators and faculty are vital to the success of HBCUs, as is our competence to raise and manage funds for these institutions.

I have participated in four presidential transitions since becoming a trustee. There is not a more critical role in the success or failure of the University than its president, and not a more challenging task for the trustees than to find one who aligns with the goals and aspirations of a particular institution.

I have served as chairman of the trustee board since 2011 and have had the privilege to coordinate consensus as we have sought to plot the vision for Virginia Union. This visioning has necessitated input from all stakeholders, students, faculty, staff, alumni, and community partners. When I think about how the grace of God has functioned in my life as it relates to Virginia Union, I am overwhelmed with gratitude. When I consider how a student who could not read received a conditional acceptance for matriculation and now thirty-five years later signs the degree for every student that graduates from the University, all I can say is, God's grace is amazing. I cannot help but say thank you in word and deed. My story is not exceptional. There are many among our alumni who have similar stories, and we are all compelled by what we have received to return and say thank you!

No reflection of grace extended to me would be adequate without acknowledging the role of the church in my life. The Black church has been in many ways the custodian of Black culture, the place which sustained us spiritually and nursed hope in our darkest days. It was a place of affirmation when the White majority demeaned us at every point, sabotaging our self-esteem. We could go to church and find self-confidence and dignity. I know that my healthy self-esteem is due in large part to my growing up under the influence of the church. Being exposed to the communal environment of the church for me was therapeutic. The sermons were affirming. Growing up in the youth activities gave me the opportunity to develop resources within myself, long before being afforded the opportunity to attend VUU.

My church experience deposited in me aspiration. It reinforced in me the notion that I could achieve. Moreover, the church gave me values and a sense of right and wrong.

It taught me to value truth and the sacredness of human life. It developed in me a moral compass.

My home church, the Community Baptist Church in West Philadelphia, was a congregation made up of people who loved the Lord. They were ordinary, hard-working families who sought to live in accordance with the values of the gospel. I came to know how to worship as they modeled worshiping before me. Many Wednesday nights, my grandmother would take me to prayer meeting. It was in those meetings that I learned how to talk to God and develop spiritual access to the eternal. I first learned of God's grace in my local church, and that knowledge has secured me. I developed an abiding appreciation for the hymns and their melodies and spiritual insights, which have warmed my heart throughout the years. It was in this context and setting that I identified a calling to ministry. My pastor was a spiritual coach and I learned much from our personal encounters. He was always an encourager.

Ultimately, I owe what I have become to the grace of God working in the life of my parents, as none of this would have been possible without them and their willingness to be obedient to the direction of God in their lives. They led me to the church and the face of God. My faith in God was cultivated by my parents and by the church. The church has given purpose and direction to my life. I love the church and have poured my life into it as a pastor for the past fifty years. My commitment and service has essentially been my offering of gratitude.

I followed the counsel of my pastor, the Reverend James Edward Hamlin, and applied for admission to Virginia Union University in 1967.

Pictured here with President Claude G. Perkins and Dr. Dorothy Eseonu before commencement. In 2010, I was elected chairman of Virginia Union Board of Directors.

In 1971 I was called to St. James Baptist Church, Henrico County, VA and continued pastoring my first congregation at Rising Mt. Zion Baptist Church, Richmond, VA.

Pastor and people of Grace Baptist Church, Mt. Vernon, NY, have continued expanding the use of our sanctuary in service to God as servants of His people for 45 years tenure.

The National Baptist Convention USA, Inc. World Center built in Nashville, Tennessee during the administration of president Dr. T. J. Jemison was dedicated, June 21, 1989.

Pictured with Dr. T. J. Jemison and board member Dr. J. Benjamin Hardwick.in Baptist World Center's conference room.

President Ronald Reagan greeting and receiving me in the Oval Office, 1984.

Hosting President George H. W. Bush at the National Baptist Convention USA, Inc., Atlanta, GA, 1992

I met with President William Jefferson Clinton often during his eight years' administration at the White House. He was the guest speaker at the National Baptist Convention USA, Inc. in New Orleans, LA, 1994.

Mrs. Richardson and I are received by President Barack Obama and First Lady Michelle Obama at the White House, Christmas 2010.

Inez and I, far right, Martin Luther King III, Rev. Al Sharpton, Congressman John Lewis, Speaker of the House of Representatives Nancy Pelosi and others, 2013 National Action Network: Realize the Dream March recognizing the 50th Anniversary of the 1963 March on Washington.

Pictured at April 2019 Presidential Candidates Forum with Stacey Abrams, former Georgia gubernatorial candidate, and president, Rev. Al Sharpton, during the National Action Network's annual convention.

Convening Conference of National Black Churches 2019

Pictured with New York Governor Andrew Cuomo and Rev. Al Sharpton.

Dedicating future witness to grace.

CHAPTER THIRTEEN

Ecumenism

I HAVE NEVER VIEWED MY DENOMINATIONAL AFFILIATION AS a basis to invalidate the authenticity of a denomination different than my own. Beyond that I have grown to respect the diversity in others' experiences and how they worship and in doing so have learned that the grace of God is not limited by His favoritism of any specific Christian denomination. It may well be that there is, in my spiritual DNA, acceptance of another's denominational choice. This may be because my mother was born in the Colored Methodist Episcopal Church and my father in the African Methodist Episcopal Church. They then married and became Baptist. I was born into a Baptist family that was not tied down to a specific choice of denomination. I believe the early posture of my family set the stage for my willingness to be involved in ecumenism.

The truth is I am essentially a Baptist Christian because my parents before me were. I am profoundly aware that if my parents before me were Presbyterian or Lutheran or even Catholic that it is highly likely that my window to God would have been different. The constant is that no matter what pathway I have traveled, at the end of the day, the grace of God has allowed me to find myself in true communion with Him. Ecumenism calls us as Christians to live beyond what we know and understand to foster closer relationships and sever the boundaries that disconnect us from each other. The scriptures illustrate how we ought to view our difference in Christ. "For as we have many members in one body, and all members have not the same office: So we, being many, are one body in Christ, and every one members one of another" (Romans 12: 4-5).

Coming to New York from the South, I became immersed in a much more tolerant and diverse faith climate than in my former pastorate in Richmond, Virginia. I immediately became part of the inter-faith clergy group in the city of Mount Vernon, thereby interacting for the first time in my ministry with leaders of various denominations and faith backgrounds. It was an opportunity to become familiar with our common interest in peace and justice. Together we found common ground to face the challenges of our community.

The opportunity to get involved beyond my denominational exclusivity and to engage in ecumenism internationally came when as general secretary I was designated to be the National Baptist Convention's representative at the convening of the World Council of Churches (WCC) in Vancouver, British Columbia, Canada. The WCC is a worldwide Christian inter-church organization founded in 1948. The WCC represents more than 590 million Christians across the world in 150 different countries, including 520,000 local congregations served by 493,000 pastors and priests.

The WCC arose out of the ecumenical movement and is based on the following statement:

> *The World Council of Churches is a*
> *fellowship of churches which confess the*
> *Lord Jesus Christ as God and Savior*
> *according to the scriptures, and therefore seek*
> *to fulfill together their common calling to the*
> *glory of God: Father, Son and Holy Spirit.*
> *It is a community of churches on the way to*
> *visible unity in one faith and one eucharistic*
> *fellowship, expressed in worship and common*
> *life of Christ. It seeks to advance towards*
> *this unity, as Jesus prayed for his followers*
> *"that the world may believe" (John 17:21).*

Being engaged with this global fellowship of Christians empowered and enlightened me. It changed my worldview and heightened my appreciation for the diversity of the modern worldwide Christian movement. As I visited with church leaders in multiple countries across six continents, my faith perspective was enlarged. I am a committed Christian, have accepted Jesus Christ as my Lord and Savior, and have been baptized and believe in the truth of John 3:16. Because of the many opportunities I had been given to experience what was the religious "norm" in other cultures, I also became more open and acknowledging of the place that non-Christian religions held in society, even if their values and beliefs did not match my own.

This awakening influenced my approach to ministry for all the years ahead. The discussions that we shared in these sessions affirmed our common belief in baptism, the Eucharist, and mission as fundamental elements of Christian unity. What an engaging experience to sit in the plenaries with headsets on, having the discussions from many languages immediately translated to English. It is to feel engaged with multiple cultures all at once. The world seemed so much smaller and inter-connected in these forums. One realizes the commonality of the human dilemma no matter our geographic location. The granular challenges of purpose, meaning, faith, and interpersonal relationships are the same.

Like the WCC, I have been affiliated with the Conference of National Black Churches (CNBC), formerly known as the Congress of National Black Churches, for more than twenty-five years. The CNBC is comprised of the national leadership of the eight largest historical Black denominations in America. The organization represents more than eighty percent of African American Christians across the USA. CNBC serves as a vehicle by which our denominations collaborate in the areas of social justice and public policy on behalf of African American communities.

I served as consultant to the board, then as vice chairman, and for the past twelve years, I have been chairman and CEO. I inherited the assignment from Bishop John Hurst Adams, the retired senior bishop of the AME church. Bishop

Adams had been a mentoring influence in the ecumenical movement among Black Christians. It was as though he was preparing me for my future leadership of the CNBC. Bishop Adams famously admonished a concept of leadership that he labeled "The Chemistry of Consultation," which continues to instruct me. He said, "No matter how great your idea, if you collaborate with others, when you are finished, you will emerge with an improved idea."

I became chairman of the conference at a time of transition in the organization— a time when the sustaining support of the Lilly Endowment was ending. In partnership with members of the board, we had to create a new model of support for CNBC, one that was more self-reliant and gave us greater freedom to address the issues of the African American community. These years have been years of great financial challenge but most impactful on our advocacy on behalf of our community. We have, in the past decade, launched initiatives at our annual consultation that have confronted racism head on and around such issues as re-emerging racial polarization and violence as seen in the killings of the "Mother Emanuel Nine," the rise of White nationalism and crimes, and the racial disparities in health care and the criminal justice system.

One of the ways we have sought to do this is by equipping our denominational leadership with accurate data on the state of racism in America. Our sessions have also sought to open up direct and honest dialogue between Black and White denominational leaders. I am particularly grateful to our sisters and brothers in the Evangelical Lutheran, United

Methodist, United Church of Christ, and Presbyterian denominations. It is an initiative that we intend to expand.

CNBC is critical to the life of Black religion in America. It is the only place where Black church leaders share discourse across denominational lines. It is where that leadership becomes familiar with one another. Moreover, it is the vehicle for collective force on behalf of our people. The impact of a truly united Black church could be enormous. I have found in this highly honored assignment a witness to grace. If one's heart is willing, God has an abundance of ways to use the gifts He has given us.

I also became the National Baptist Convention's representative to the National Council of Churches (NCC). It was a further opportunity to engage in ecumenical dialogue from a national perspective. The National Council of Churches of Christ in the USA is the largest ecumenical body in the United States. The NCC is an ecumenical partnership of thirty-eight Christian faith groups in the United States.

After some years of not being directly involved with the NCC, yet remaining akin to its goals and objectives of Christian Unity in our nation and the world, I was elected an at-large member of their board. I have always admired those who have given themselves to the work of ecumenism. I think it is one of the most noble and essential vocations of ministry. I take great pride in one of the daughters of the ministry of Grace Baptist Church, the Reverend Dr. Leslie Copeland-Tune, who has made a career in ecumenism. I have been blessed each time I encounter her in the pursuit of helping us to see the church as one in the face of obstructive realities. She is the chief operating officer of the NCC and has earned a reputation as an outstanding ecumenist.

Moreover, I salute the leadership efforts of my younger colleague, Bishop Dr. W. Darin Moore, a native of the city of Mount Vernon and former pastor of Greater Centennial A.M.E. Zion Church. He was an effective force in the cause of global and national ecumenism as he has served as chairman of the NCC. He has also played an active role in the witness of the Conference of National Black Churches. I have found that sometimes our inspiration to go forward flows from those who have preceded us, and my life has been blessed by many of those I have made reference to on these pages. However, there are times when those who are younger than us inspire us to fresh frontiers. That is my relationship with Bishop Moore. To see young people who emerge from the ministry as church leaders, pastors, seminary professors, preachers, and Christian leaders in multiple fields of endeavor is to witness grace.

As a part of my ecumenical efforts, I recently gave an address to the National Council of Churches for the 400-year observance of American slavery. The meeting was convened at Point Comfort, Virginia, the site where twenty-one Africans disembarked in 1619, initiating the institution of slavery in America. It was, in my opinion, a relevant display on behalf of the NCC to prick the conscience of the broader church community of the continuing consequence of slavery and America's original sin of racism. The White Christian church must own its complicity in and its profiting from the enslavement of Black people. The words that follow come from this address.

I am humbled by this opportunity to share with you, my sisters and brothers in Christ. All of us are summoned here from different faith communities and diverse backgrounds. We are Black and White, male and female, yet we are united in the cause of justice. Regretfully, we are gathered at this place negotiating the reality of America's original sin, and her continuing shame and pain. We are here, in our diversity, within a tapestry of hope. As we stand with this backdrop of human misery and shame—the misery of the enslaved and the shame of the enslaver—I, nevertheless, feel encouraged by the fact that we have gathered here together in observance of the continuing impact of this awful chapter in American history.

We are here today both to remember and to lament! To this place, we have come with solemn sadness—to this very place where the cruel system of American slavery was birthed. We, the sons and daughters of the enslaved and the enslavers, have gathered and come to this place where the long procession of systemic dehumanization of men and women began in this country, a dehumanization based on skin color and fueled by greed. This place has been and is a place of human bondage. The trees, the hills, the rivers, and the roads stand as silent witnesses to an indescribable cruelty that took place in this space. I believe, if we listen hard with our hearts, in this moment, we can hear the slaves —their voices, their lament, their cries, and their tortured groans.

I want to suggest that today we should, each one of us, do four things as a counter response to the fact that enslavers owned Africans, in order to lead us down a pathway of hope. The first thing we must do here, today, is own slavery as a reality. Slavery is not a fable. The stories of slavery are not fairy tales. It actually happened. Real human beings were tortured, raped, mutilated, humiliated, lynched, and murdered. Enslaved people were seen not as people at all but as commodities to be bought, sold, and exploited. We can never understand the depth of slavery's degradation until we have disengaged ourselves from the slave master's definitions.

American slavery is about exploiting, raping, lynching, and killing real children, women, and men. It is about dissolving family structures and inflicting psychological pain. It is a cruelty that cannot be overstated. It is often referred to as the worst form of human bondage in the history of the world. Yet, we have gathered today to own it afresh. It may be hard to put our heads around the fact that we, together, are both the heirs of those who committed this gross inhumane treatment and the sons and daughters of the victims of this mass cruelty. As a Black man, I not only feel grief in this moment for my ethnic forebears, but I also feel deep sadness over mankind's ability to disregard humanity. We must, in the spirit of remembrance and lamentation, attempt to visit this reality in our minds. To step back into this reality is a deeply despairing experience, but, if here and now, we fail to own the reality of slavery, we miss the pregnant opportunity to exploit this moment.

The depth of slavery's cruelty is captured in the stories of the enslaved. Such is the case in a statement made by Mum Bett (Elizabeth Freeman) as told in an article in the *New York Times*. She captured the essence of the slave experience, while lobbying for her freedom, in this single line, "If one minute's freedom had been offered to me, and I had been told I must die at the end of that minute, I would have taken it."

Frederick Douglass, when speaking as an abolitionist to White audiences in North America and in Europe, opened the window for them to observe the cruelty of what it was like to be a slave when he offered up his whip-torn back as a testimony to that harsh reality.

Secondly, we must own the church's complicity in slavery, racism, and discrimination. Christians would do well to build an altar here in Virginia and at other places. We should begin at the Vatican, England, Portugal, Spain, France, and the Netherlands to confess and seek a way to rectify the pain they have inflicted upon the people of this diaspora. The fact is that the progenitor and sustainer of the enslavement of Africans was the Christian church. Mary Elliott and Jazmine Hughes described the church's involvement in the 1619 Project, published by The New York Times. "In the 15th century, the Roman Catholic Church divided the world in half, granting Portugal a monopoly on trade in West Africa and Spain the right to colonize the New World in its quest for land and gold. Pope Nicholas V buoyed Portuguese efforts and issued the Romanus Pontifex of 1455, which affirmed Portugal's exclusive rights to territories it claimed along the west African coast including the proceeds of trade from those areas. It granted the rights to invade, plunder, and reduce their persons to perpetual slavery."

During this enslavement, many Christian churches adopted an accommodating theology for the practice of slavery—a practice which continued after the emancipation, into the Jim Crow era, and beyond.

Clergy produced extravagant eisegesis to accommodate the slave masters, who were members and leaders of their congregations. More devastating was the silence of the church at a time when something needed to be said. The pulpits of White congregations knew better but had no prophetic courage to speak or to act. The good news is that, while the White church was silent and disengaged and advocating against slavery, the spirit of Christ was alive and well among the enslaved, birthing a faith of survival and liberation. It was a defiant faith in the midst of oppression. This defiant faith showed up in their theology and in their musicology. The enslaver's preacher would show up and quote a safe, docile scripture, like "Slaves, obey your masters," or "God has ordained your master to rule over you," but the enslaved would go worship by night in the brush harbor and quote an antiphonal response to the slave master's scripture: "so if the son sets you free, you will be free indeed" (John 8:36) or "there is neither Jew nor Gentile, there is neither slave nor free, there is neither male or female, for ye are all one in Christ Jesus" (Galatians 3:28). In addition, the music sung by the enslaved defied the context of their oppression. In the grip of slavery, with trouble all about them, and no existential evidence of things getting better, with defiant hope they sang, "I am so glad trouble don't last always." While the organized church was absent, Jesus was in the slave camp.

In the third instance, we must own the consequences of slavery and racism. The last sentence on the historical marker at Point Comfort, where the first Africans disembarked, reads, "the United States abolished slavery in 1865."

Nothing could be further from the truth. Slavery continues in the form of racism. Racism is a byproduct of slavery. When slavery ended, it metamorphosed into racism. The legacy of American slavery is American racism, and racism is the legitimate child of slavery.

The ancient prophet Jeremiah, upon assessing the state of Israel during a continuing crisis in the 5th century BC, spoke words that align with the situation of Black people today. He said, "The harvest is past, the summer is ended, and we are not saved." African Americans can't help but feel the collateral damage of 246 years of slavery and 151 years of overt and covert racism. The fallout of slavery still stigmatizes Black existence in America. No matter what an African American may achieve, he or she is never far from the negative consequences of being Black in America.

All of the systems of America measure a conscious bias against Black people. According to a Pew Foundation report published this year, "most Americans say the legacy of slavery still affects Black people in the U.S. today." The median wealth of White households is 20 times that of Black households. There are many continuing vestiges of racism in the day-to-day lives of African Americans, from as subtle an incident as a Black man waiting for his car at a valet stand and a White person walking up and handing him their key or a Black man entering an elevator whereupon the White woman grasps her purse tightly. These are not fables. They are instances I have personally experienced. Moreover, there are inequalities executed on a daily basis in our criminal justice system. Just recently, a Black homeless mother who sent her six-year-old to a better school in the wrong town was jailed for five years while a White wealthy mother was sentenced to 10 days in jail for participating in the college admissions scandal.

A recent report found that Black men are six times more likely to be incarcerated than White men. The economic statistics are equally revealing of the continuing impact of systemic racism. Blacks are three times more likely to live in poverty. Blacks earn thirty-five percent less than Whites at the median. It is generally known that in every measure of the quality of life in America, Blacks are at the bottom when compared to Whites, Asians, and Hispanics. Whether we are speaking about incarceration, education, health, or economics, the negative legacy of slavery is irrefutable. Not only has the legacy of slavery inflicted Black people physiologically and sociologically, but it has affected Blacks psychologically as well. The damage of our collective self-esteem and self-confidence is directly connected to us internalizing inferiority. It is what Dr. Joy DeGruy refers to in her book as Post Traumatic Slave Syndrome. It is America's legacy of enduring injury and healing—the fallout of slavery on a whole group of people.

Finally, we must own a meaningful response to the residue of slavery and the continuing violence of racism. There is only one response for the Black church and the White church. It is a joint assignment. Unfortunately, part of the destructive consequence of racism is that we see ourselves as Black and White; we must find a way to see our difference as an opportunity to celebrate our diversity like one who walks through a flower garden appreciating the diversity of colors, shapes and sizes without assigning stigma or guilt. The rose is beautiful, but so is the mum, as is the daisy, and together, they make a garden. The goal of the church is to make the world a garden. The question that begs to be asked is, "How do we do that?"

I am not sure! However, I am sure that we are the only ones who have that assignment. Both Black and White Christians will have to figure out how to fulfill this mandate. It will require soul searching, repentance, repair, sacrifice, and grace. It will not be easy, but, if we are sincere, God will be with us because He gave us this assignment. "Be thou reconciled." We are called to be gardeners, to make all the flowers healthy and to celebrate the value of each. Our collective response must be restless and relentless to eliminate the stain of racism from our culture.

In the gospels, Jesus speaks of the young rich ruler who, in order to inherit the kingdom, had to sell all his riches and come and follow Jesus. I am not sure that it was giving up his riches that made him leave Jesus, but maybe it was following Jesus that he could not handle. Following Jesus is hard! In the case of racism, Black Christians will have to truly forgive the White church. That is hard! And White Christians will have to repair the damage done by 400 years of slavery and racism. That will be hard. We will have to help each other with our assignment, and that will be hard. But it is hard to follow Jesus!

We Christians are called to live with a righteous indignation regarding social injustice. Awareness of systemic racism and the legacy of slavery ought to leave us radically disturbed by the conduct of the current president of the United States, disturbed by the resurgence of overt white supremacy, disturbed by the continuing inequalities grounded in racism, disturbed by the criminal justice system. We who are Jesus's people ought to be known as the fellowship of the disturbed, the restless, the determined. I must confess that I have little hope in our institutions and systems of government without an external insistence driven by the force of higher values.

I have little hope in corporate entities to remove the stain of America's original sin as a priority above capital gains. I have little hope in the resident good of our humanity to subsume our selfishness and greed. But the hope I do have is in the transformative power of the Gospel to change the hearts of men and women, to dismantle the systems of oppression. My sentiment is adequately appropriated in the words of the 19th century pastor, Edward Mote, who wrote:

> *My hope is built on nothing less*
> *than Jesus' blood and righteousness. I dare*
> *not trust the sweetest frame,*
> *but holy lean on Jesus name.*
> *On Christ the solid rock I stand;*
> *all other ground is sinking sand.*
> *When darkness hides His loving face I rest*
> *on His unchanging grace.*
> *In every high and stormy gale*
> *my anchor holds within the veil.*
> *On CHRIST ...*

CHAPTER FOURTEEN

The Strange Ways of God

As I gaze back over my journey, there are a plethora of emotions I have felt when confronted by the actions of God—grief, fear, anxiety, anger, disappointment, confusion, and despair. These emotions, when attributed to God, have caused me to question Him.

The great interrogator of God in the biblical text is Job. When faced with catastrophe, Job confronts God and demands that God explain Himself. The desire to interrogate God in the face of unexplainable and disappointing circumstances is what I call the "Jobian Syndrome." When faced with the strange ways of God, each of us is tempted to ask God, "Why?"

There have been times in my life when my thoughts have been invaded by the Jobian Syndrome. The times that I asked God *why* were undergirded by fear, or anger or disappointment. What I have discovered is that the scriptures are still true. Isaiah 55:8 reads, "For my thoughts are not your thoughts, neither are your ways my ways, saith the LORD."

The 17th-century composer William Cowper was right when he wrote, "God moves in mysterious ways His wonders to perform; He plants His footsteps in the sea and rides upon the storm." I have come to discover that God will put you out to bring you in, let you lose so you can win, make you sick to get you well, put you down to pull you up. God's logic is upside down when juxtaposed with human logic.

The landscape of my journey has had highs and lows, peaking mountains and sloping valleys. We can never know or understand the mind of God. We can only trust Him. Even though I questioned God more than a few times, God's strange ways still worked for my good.

Recently I felt this the most when my son shared with me that he decided to accept his call to ministry in the midst of the confusion of the NBC election. He reminded me of a conversation we had in the aftermath of the election that ended in my defeat. He admitted that the outcome of the election and the process that sealed my defeat left him feeling dejected. He could not understand how dishonorable actions could triumph over honorable actions. He felt disillusioned and grew unwilling to consider a life of ministry. However, I told him, "Our relationship with God is not defined by whether we win or lose, and through our failures we find our true strength.

Our failure is not God's failure. When you are mistreated, it is not a time to abandon your faith." Unbeknownst to me at the time, these words helped redirect him. In the midst of all of the chaos during that time God was still speaking to my son, and my son was surrendering to God. Because I moved on from that defeat, encouraged in that place of failure, God moved on with me, and I moved on with God!

As I have grown older, the strange ways of God have appeared more readily to me. Two and a half years ago I was in Miami with my dear brother in ministry Dwight Jones and our sons, Brent, Derrick, and William when a call came from my doctor in New York. I previously had an MRI to determine if I had prostate cancer. However, the doctor informed me that they had discovered something in my liver while examining the MRI that looked very serious. The doctor wanted me to return to the hospital to have a biopsy procedure completed on my liver, which I did.

They discovered that I had a tumor the size of a tennis ball in my liver, but they couldn't determine if it was malignant or if it would have to be removed. After further review, the medical team concluded that it was not malignant, but due to its size, it needed to be removed in the short term. My surgeon, Dr. William Jernigan, assured me that I would be able to resume my activities fully in three months or less. Even though Dr. Jernigan's confidence was reassuring, I still had lingering fear, but I knew that I needed to hold on to God's hand even tighter in spite of my situation.

I made plans for my absence from the church for three months. Several of my close colleagues from across the nation and nearby agreed to fill the pulpit. Among them were Dwight C. Jones, Howard John Wesley, Ralph Douglas

West, Carl Washington, Al Sharpton, and Adolphus Lacey. The staff and leadership stepped up, and the church was prepared for this season of challenge.

My family and staff were with me as I was being prepared for surgery. At a certain point the curtain at the foot of my bed was pulled back. To my delight it was Alexandria Lewis, one of the former youths of our church. "Good morning, Pastor," she said. "I am an anesthesiologist here at Memorial Sloan Kettering. I have reviewed your needs, and I have shared that you are my pastor. We will take good care of you." At that moment, as far as I was concerned, there stood a beautiful ebony angel. As tears of joy trickled down my cheeks, I thought about the many Sundays she sat in the pew. This young doctor was a graduate of Yale Medical School and was one of the youths who had been active in our ministry and a part of our Ministry of College and Career Alliance (MOCCA). Now she was watching over me! I had no idea that she was on staff at the hospital.

As they rolled me down the long corridor to the surgical suite, I had time to thank God one more time and to surrender myself totally into His hands. What a gift of grace! If I had not had the MRI, the sizable tumor in my liver would not have been discovered. God's pathway to our future is not always our pathway, but His way is sure.

These episodes, among others, clearly depict the grace of God functioning in my life and in the life of those dear to me, even in the midst of disappointment and confusion. I have come to know failure, disappointment, and defeat as preparation for future assignments. The positive collateral consequence of failure may very well be that it sets one up to know the sovereign power of God more intimately and to depend on Him to lead the way. Oh, the strange ways of God!

Hope, Justice, and Reconciliation

THERE IS AN ABIDING REALITY IN AMERICA THAT DIMINISHES the potential for this republic to fulfill its promise. The scourge of racism is deeply embedded in American culture and seems to be extremely resistant to elimination. I begin this discourse by addressing racism first because it is all invasive in the lives of people of color. Every other issue of Black life in America is impacted by it. Therefore, we must assume that people of color will be dealing with this serious obstacle to opportunity for a very long time to come. It does not mean we will be denied progress, but it will be a constant push against a headwind, requiring more from us than our White counterparts.

In recent days, the hidden hate residing in pockets of America's collective consciousness has resurfaced, emboldened by the rhetoric and policies of the Trump administration. A significant segment of White Americans carry the poison of racial hate in their hearts. Let me hasten to say the obvious: not every White person is racist. Yet, every White person benefits from the privilege that is the consequence of systemic racism, and every Black person is disadvantaged by it.

While visible, nonviolent protest must remain in our arsenal as we verbally and visibly reject injustice, we must continue to equip ourselves with preparation and determination to overcome the disadvantages that are the byproduct of racist attitudes. This is the formula our forebears employed as they struggled for progress in the face of overt, covert, and systemic racism. Those who fail to understand the importance of education, positive self-esteem, honesty, moral integrity, and civility will guarantee themselves a seat among those who are cast aside. Yet, these things alone will not assure that you will be immune from the venom of racism as it seeks to impede your progress.

Our great legacy of achievement by Black men and women in the face of obstruction is pure testimony that we can still succeed, and we must. There is much encouragement to move forward and upward. The Black preacher and the Black church must view it as a sacred responsibility to encourage, inform, and empower this generation and the next, so that we may fulfill the ambitions of our ancestors in acquiring total inclusion into American society.

The challenge for the pulpit going forward is to be totally informed, courageous, prepared, and passionate—a voice for those who have no voice.

The election of Barack Obama was in many ways the fulfillment of those things I had struggled to see achieved;

it was unexpected joy. In his ascendency, I discovered a patriotism of which I did not know I was capable. I felt, for a moment, fully American. While we had been to the White House many times during other administrations, when Inez and I went at the invitation of First Lady Michelle and President Obama, it was as though it was our first time. The very presence of a successful Black president quieted the critics' claim of Black inferiority.

Unfortunately, the desire for people throughout the world to spew hate towards others who are not like them exists in many forms, and the issues surrounding gender discrimination and human sexuality are no longer only at the door of the Black church, but on the altar. The challenge to understanding the church's position on same-sex, loving relationships based on biblical interpretations among some in the Black community is highly sought after, while on the other hand the church's dogma is dismissed by others. Our sons and daughters have an openness to these realities of humanity that generations before did not speak about but were always present. I think that unbiased open discourse in the Black church about sexuality ought to be welcomed, aiding the church in gaining greater relevance among young people. Yes, transparency and relevance must be priorities for the Black church if it is to avoid the fate of becoming relics of history as its counterparts through Europe. Our Jesus can stand the scrutiny of science, the query of the young, and the pursuit of change, and He must. As a matter of fact, these current dynamics may push us closer to the heart of Christ's message.

Recently I had two young women approach me at the close of worship and ask, "When the time comes, Pastor, would you perform our marriage?"

To which I replied, "When the time comes, we should discuss it."

One was a very active, long-term member of our congregation, and the other would eventually become a member. Their question threw me for a loop. I hope it did not show on my face. This was the first time I was confronted with the issue of same-sex marriage in the church.

I have had several conversations with clergy colleagues about the prospect of being requested to perform same-sex marriage ceremonies. It caused me to examine any previously held opinions I had regarding the matter. The fact that my brother was gay has sensitized me to the pain and isolation that discrimination causes in the life of a same-sex, loving individual.

My point here is not to exhaust the conversation around this issue, but rather to point out that people in the pew are more diverse in their thinking than ever and what is emerging, for better or worse, is a new tolerance and transparency. The question going forward that the church will have to ask itself and seek an answer to is, "What would Jesus do?" What is required first and foremost by a Christian is to reflect the attitude of Christ. These questions challenge traditions, customs, practices, and preferences as much or more than theology.

Ultimately the Black church, being intimately acquainted with the evil of hatred, must be an aggressive agent of love. The victimization of African Americans in this country gives the Black church moral authority to speak out and compels it to act. The current polarization of Americans on the basis of human difference must not be tolerated at any level. The Black church must be the leading opponent of hate in any form, anywhere!

Part of these changes have been spurred on by the impact of digitalization. Digitalization has affected education, communication, transportation, healthcare, and banking and has far-reaching consequences for all segments of the population. The Black community, its churches, and its other institutions are not excluded. Often the Black community has been a victim of the digital divide. The lack of access to computers continues, albeit to a lesser degree, to be an obstacle to enabling our community through the internet. One of the benefits of certain technologies is its nonracial identification of users, thereby avoiding the opportunity for racial bias.

Technology has created a totally different mindset that fosters the lack of socialization. Recently we shared a family dinner with my children and grandchildren at one of the restaurants nearby our home. There were eleven of us. Even before placing our orders, from the youngest to the oldest we were consumed with our devices. I collected all of the devices so we could share some quality time together. Technology is threatening our intimacy, and that is a challenge for the church as it seeks to foster spirituality. The devaluing of interpersonal relationships has an unintentional consequence on the fabric of our culture. The invading access to technology is having a rising impact on how we worship given the prevalence of video streaming and online giving. It is so invasive that churches must embrace it; technology will have an ever-increasing impact on the worship space. The orientation of the coming generations will require it. It is transforming lifestyles and our institutions will be required to adjust for survival. The invention of robots and artificial intelligence will impact job opportunities and lifestyle choices and the church will not be outside its wake.

How we receive education and information has been greatly altered by the formation of the new digital landscape. The democratization of information has made it readily available to all classes of our society. The Black church must lead our community to exploit this opportunity to its fullest. Moreover, preachers must maximize this tool to assure the accuracy of the message he/she brings. There is no room in our emerging reality for misinformed leadership. It is too costly. We must hold ourselves to a higher standard of excellence.

The criminal justice system in the United States is the modern extension of the bonds of slavery wrapping its ugly grasp around Black men in particular and people of color in general. It serves to oppress Black men to the benefit of huge economic corporate interests. Corporations and government entities are co-conspirators in facilitating these disproportionately high incarceration rates among people of color, especially young Black men, which in and of itself is a high crime. The current prison system deprives Black families of fathers, sons, brothers, and uncles while tagging them with unbearable stigma. We must resist the dehumanization of prisoners while welcoming those who are restorable back into our homes, our communities, and our churches. We cannot afford the brain drain and overwhelming loss of men from our families that the current penal policies inflict unfairly upon people of color. This is the challenge which will abide with us and restrict us going into the next century and must be addressed.

The lack of access to competent legal representation, the insistence on unfair bail release, and insensitive justices all serve to awaken in each of us a conscious unfairness, leading to a further sense of constraints that serves to foster further oppression. It is what Michelle Alexander so aptly refers to as "The new Jim Crow." The criminal justice system lies at the center of our ability to restore our fathers and our sons. This reality is so threatening to our future that the church must act responsively. Something is clearly out of focus when Blacks are twelve percent of the general population and eighty percent of the prison population.

The church must speak out, affirming the dignity of the incarcerated, and call on the powers that be to set the captives free. The Black church must actively assist in dismantling "the cradle to prison pipeline." The fifth chapter of Mark records the story of a man in chains, who had been possessed by demons and considered crazy by his community, but he had sense enough to seek Jesus! Jesus freed him from the demons and the chains. When the community saw him clothed and in his right mind, the Bible says, "they were afraid." They were not afraid until he was in his right mind, free from the demons and the chains. We must free our sons and daughters from the demons which constrict them and the chains that bind them so that they may actualize their God-given potential! When we do, the oppressors will fear them.

The Black church must be prepared for the shifting landscape of values among our youth that may not align with traditional Christian principles. The church will find itself serving the community in a more religiously diverse context. There was a time when, if you met an African American, he would identify with one of four faith expressions; he was either Baptist, Methodist, Pentecostal, or occasionally Catholic. Today, the community has become much more diverse to include those who identify with no faith expression. In my early years, everyone owned a religious tag whether they practiced it or not.

Traditional religions no longer necessarily have an inherited advantage from one generation to the other. Moreover, this generation is making its own choices based on an individual congregational profile without regard to regional or national identity. Contributing to this diversity is transcultural interactions fostered by a growing national diversity and expedited geographical access, the result of improved transportation and communications between global entities. The world is a shrinking global community, impacting all communities through increased exposure to each other. The Black church, going forward, must include this reality in its calculus as it seeks growth.

Gentrification, migration, shifting labor opportunities, changing demographics, and personal interracial and intercultural relationships all add to the changes in the context of the pew of the Black church. Added to this is a diminishing racial loyalty and a rising self-centered focus that lies more on "me" than "we." Beyond these challenges catalogued above, the core issues of our humanity, such as faith, spirituality, hope, grace, suffering, life, and death are confronted by all, regardless of contextual considerations.

These issues and more must inform the content that flows from the pulpit if the church is to actualize its promise. The challenge for the preacher is to capture the voice of God and His essence in his/her declaration; to do that is to experience the penultimate gift of grace, that we His lowly servants would be so blessed to be conduits of His will. Articulating His call to reconciliation, His aspiration for justice as we live in hope. It is what the prophet Micah declared when speaking on God's behalf: "...and what doth the Lord require of thee, but to do justly, and to love mercy, and to walk humbly with thy God?"

A Voiceless Ministry

THERE IS A DIFFERENCE BETWEEN KEEPING SILENT AND LOSING one's voice. Keeping silent is a choice that an individual makes. However, losing one's voice is involuntary. Losing one's voice renders an individual incapable of saying anything.

Losing your voice means you cannot speak and no one is able to listen to what you have to say. Voicelessness makes you a nonentity—invisible. Without a voice you do not matter, and you have no presence. Voicelessness is not the mere absence of speech; it is the loss of impact.

The Black church suffers today from various levels or degrees of voicelessness. Led by preachers who have lost their voice and ministers who wear vestments but have no voice, the Black church's perspective is unheard, and her people are not heard in public policy discourse. We who were once vocal and dominant in the civil rights arena have become silent and anemic. It is not that we are not making noise, but the noise we are making is often nonsensical. We are not speaking about the pain our people are feeling.

The King Herods and Pharaohs of our day have inflicted pain and systemic exclusion on our people, and we preachers have been silent. A former mentor of mine once said, "A silent friend, when something ought to be said, is worse than a deadly enemy."

The biases of our judicial system have incarcerated our sons and daughters in disproportionate numbers, assisted by a cradle to prison pipeline that is committed to misdirecting our future. We have lost our voice!

The era of Trump has ushered in a resurgence of overt racism, which has emboldened white supremacists, Ku Klux Klansmen and Nazi sympathizers. Right wing judges in this nation's highest courts are lined up to reverse groundbreaking laws for which our forebears gave their lives. The defunding of public schools is a co-conspiratorial action to assure the dysfunction of masses of people of color, ensuring that the cradle to prison pipeline remains intact.

We, like Zechariah, attend to the affairs of religion: we serve the altar, and we are robed in the vestments of tradition, but we have lost our voice. We may very well be righteous and compliant with the laws of our faith tradition, but we have lost our voice. The interaction between Zechariah and the angel Gabriel is instructive for those of us who may have lost our voices. Zechariah and his wife, Elizabeth, were blameless and righteous, but they lived with the social shame of being childless. They prayed about it, and God answered their prayer. He sent Gabriel to the altar to announce to Zechariah that a son (to be named John) would be born to him and his formerly barren wife. When told this news, Zechariah asks the question "How can I be sure?"

Gabriel responds, "I am Gabriel, and I stand in the presence of God! But because of your unbelief, you will not be able to speak until the announcement has been fulfilled."

There appears to be three contributing reasons for God's decision to take Zechariah's voice: fear, expectation, and no faith.

When Zechariah saw the angel at the altar he was afraid. Fear will make you lose your voice. Many of us are afraid of facing the ramifications of speaking truth to power. We are more afraid of Pharaoh than we are of God. Some of us belong to Pharaoh. We receive a check from Pharaoh and are afraid we will lose our stipend if we speak out against Pharaoh. Still, others of us are afraid to stand out as rabble rousers for fear that speaking out will sully our reputation. Don't forget, Jesus was a rabble-rouser!

Zechariah's inability to incite change meant that he had prayed but he had no expectation that his prayer would or could be answered. Many of us exercise the rhetoric of prayer but have no faith that the prayers we pray will be answered. We engage in the ritual of prayer, exercise the liturgical language, and assume the posture of prayer, yet we have zero expectation that our prayer will be answered. Zechariah could not expect God to bless him because he was focused on his limits and not God's limitlessness. All he could see was his age and the fact that his wife was barren, which drained him of any expectation that his prayer could or would be answered. How many times have we missed our blessing because we are focused on the enormity of our problem instead of the sovereignty of our God?

This shows that Zechariah had no faith. The angel Gabriel says that it is because of his unbelief that he will have no voice. Friends, you can't speak for God without first having faith in God. Faith is the fuel of biblical protest against injustice.

Isaiah spoke for God and gave us this wonderful assurance: "When thou passest through the waters, I will be with thee; and through the rivers, they will not overflow thee: when thou walkest through the fire, thou shalt not be burned; and neither shall the flame kindle upon thee." (Isaiah 43:2).

George A. Young further articulated this great truth in 1903, stating:

*In shady, green pastures, so rich and
so sweet,
God leads his dear children along;
Where the water's clear flow bathes the
weary one's feet,
God leads His dear children along.
Some through waters, some through the flood,
Some through the fire, but all through
the blood;
Some through great sorrow, but God gives
a song,
In the night season and all the day
long. ("God Leads Us Along")*

The Hebrew boys, Shadrach, Meshach, and Abednego spoke truth to King Nebuchadnezzar on the fringe of the furnace fueled by faith in God! Nathan the prophet spoke truth to King David in ridicule of the injustice put upon Uriah, the husband of his mistress. Propelled by a certain faith in God's thirst for righteousness and justice, Paul and Silas were beaten, jailed, stoned, and later martyred for speaking truth to power. Compelled by unwavering faith in God, Stephen gave voice to a believing minority, being stoned while gazing upwards to heaven. The Bible says heaven stood up in acknowledgement of his great faith. Dr. Martin Luther King Jr. was a faith-driven modern prophet who spoke with clarity, precision, and power against 300 years of systemic racism. He said, "The arc of the moral universe is long, but it bends toward justice." All these servants were unafraid. They believed that God would answer prayers and had strong faith in God, and, as a consequence, they had a voice.

We are called to go into the darkness, not knowing the outcome but trusting completely in the promise of God! And I tell you, faith will give us a voice. Faith overcomes fear. Faith gives us the courage to speak truth to power. We are not alone!

Epilogue: Discovering Grace in Pandemic

As I was preparing to send my completed book manuscript to the publisher, the wave of the Coronavirus rolled across the shores to America and delayed the publication and release. It provided an unexpected opportunity to observe the presence of grace in the midst of a global pandemic. I entered this season anxious to discern the grace of God in the face of the virus. I was not disappointed.

My first response was disbelief, followed by anxiety and fear. After settling my spirit, I began to seek the face of God in this dilemma. I, like others of this generation, had never seen such a crisis, surprised by its aggressive, persistent, and inclusive impact on all humanity—how it touched every continent, nation, state, city, town, and village, eliminating the artificial boundaries of geography, nationalism, race, and religion and by so doing causing us to reevaluate how we view ourselves and others. It confronted us through glimpses of our common fragility and vulnerability.

The reflective impact of the pandemic on me is that it summoned me to introspection both collective and personal. It began with questions stirred in my spirit. Questions such as: Could it be that the grace of God could very well be manifested in this virus as an act of restoration? Could this be divine intervention for a global community that was spiraling to elimination? Is this a global reset in the face of cosmic extinction, a global purging? Was this pandemic built into the DNA of creation? Did the Cosmic Shepherd place a divine sensor in the framework of creation that would overload when predetermined levels of corruption were reached that would trigger reset actions to avoid certain destruction of the planet? Could our collective human behavior have warranted such a bold act of grace to deliver us from ourselves? Could it be because of our decadent consumption of nature's resources, our imbalanced distribution of global wealth, our ecological abuse of the planet, our inter-global conflict, our artificial barriers of differences among people in the world? Could political corruption, misplaced values, the advance of racism, classism, and flagrant disregard for social justice more than meet the criteria for global reset among human beings?

It appears that other elements of creation are untouched by this reset. The sun yet rises each morning, oceans have not lost their rhythm, seasonal cycles remain in sequence, the wind yet blows, the moon, the lantern of the night, still glows and the stars still twinkle. Have you noticed that birds yet sing and flowers are still blooming? Dogs still bark and cows are mooing. Is this readjustment directed toward humanity? Might the reset serve as an act of grace to salvage humankind from self-destructive tendencies, or an ingrained response to a humanity that has lost its way? Are these questions not worth consideration?

While we question the brokenness of our humanity, we have seen in these turbulent times signs of redeeming grace—glimpses of hope and displays of selfless concern for other human beings. This crisis has unearthed the best in us and brought to the forefront hidden compassion. We have been amazed by extraordinary acts of grace practiced amongst us. We have seen it in the exceptional sacrifices of our doctors, nurses, and health care workers. We have seen it in essential workers who risk their lives to provide the infrastructure for society to function and move towards collective healing.

We have seen selflessness as the inspiration of what we as a people can collectively become. We have seen this grace in food suppliers who generously give to those who have no food. We have seen it in congregations full of compassion equipping themselves to provide resources and to share love. We have heard a call for grace to diminished barriers that normally separate us from each other and prevent us from seeing ourselves as one global community. At the same time, we see our individual survival as a gift of grace.

We behold the unending processions of our dead to the cemetery, without pause for ritual or celebration, without "goodbye" regardless of status or wealth. This reality caused the rise of the second group of questions. What are our priorities? What really matters? When and where does life end? What have we taken for granted? Where is God? This pandemic has placed these issues of mortality in the forefront of our reflection.

I look at my grandchildren and see them as the repository of the legacy of the collaborative nurturing of our ancestors, a byproduct of grace. I recognize that we are all heirs to our past as they shall be to us. This season of "shelter in place" is the result of an aggressive, unpredictable pandemic and a poorly managed response, created by a time of lockdown and disconnection, resulting in loss of freedom and fellowship, giving rise to an unavoidable deep reflection, an occasion to refocus.

A new normal has emerged inclusive of virtual engagement, uncertainty, anxiety, insecurity, a collapsing economy, heightened polarization, essential and nonessential demarcations. There is rising desperation as evidenced in expanding food pantries, empty grocery shelves, cash supplements to individual citizens and businesses. The government is attempting to reinforce the crumbling economic foundations, while historic unemployment rates move upward each week, while at the same time seeking to understand the virus and find a cure or vaccine for it.

Amidst the haze of these turbulent times I found comfort in my own introspective reassessment of my priorities, mortality, and spirituality. The experience of the pandemic has had an impact on my perspective. I have never felt my ministry more essential, my preaching more vital, the scriptures more relevant, counseling more crucial, caring more needed, my family more valued, each day more precious, my life more useful, prayer more powerful, or God more intimately, than I have in the midst of this pandemic— all a gift of God!

Since God has extended our existence, the ultimate questions are: Did we learn the big lessons from what we have experienced? Will we hurriedly return to the same practices and values we embraced pre-pandemic? Have we learned from the pain? Will we indeed start up again or will we start over?

Black Lives Matter

The experience and isolation of the pandemic set the stage for much of America to have a fresh awakening to the current effects of racism. The seclusion and vulnerability of America caused its attention to be arrested by the recurring image of George Floyd gasping for his last breath under the knee of an unrelenting White police officer, which set loose massive protests across our nation and around the world. Thereby giving rise to the Black Lives Matter Movement (BLMM) that had been incubating in the Black community of America for months. The response by Whites in every sector of American life has been positively overwhelming. From Whites partnering with Blacks on the streets of our cities to major corporate grants intended to help repair the damage of four-hundred years of institutionalized racism.

I am cautiously hopeful that this current consciousness does not quickly dissipate. It is clearly evident to me that the intersection of the pandemic and the Black Lives Matter Movement is an act of grace, divinely orchestrated.

Appendix

Bishop John R. Bryant, retired, former senior bishop and presiding prelate, Fourth Episcopal District of the African Methodist Episcopal Church

I have known W. Franklyn Richardson for over forty years. I have known him as a disciplined seminarian, a productive pastor, a community and national moral, spiritual, and human rights leader. He is a skilled and creative man of God who knows how to bring people together and keep them together to accomplish some very impressive things. As a preacher/orator, he is listed among the most prophetic. But in his new work, *Witness to Grace: A Testimony of Favor*, he eloquently and generously shares with the reader what a powerful gift grace has been in his life. This is a must read. I found it extremely helpful and I know you will agree.

Bishop C. Nathan Edwers, pastor, Friendship UFW Baptist Church, Mt. Vernon, New York

Thirty-one years ago, January 13, 1989, I was elected pastor of Little Friendship Unified Free Will Baptist Church, now known as Friendship UFW Baptist Church. After I arrived in Mount Vernon, New York, Dr. Richardson reached out to me and began thirty-one years of mentorship and friendship. He advised me on four key issues that I needed to place on my list to accomplish: finish school, move my family out of the church parsonage and buy my own home, reach out beyond Mount Vernon to build my ministry presence, and use every opportunity possible to shed light on what God is doing through you. All of which I have done, including earning a doctoral degree in theology.

He offered instructions and advice that I heard and responded appropriately through his guidance over time. He has been in my life during the most significant moments of my children's growth, including Eric's birth. He shepherded me through my parents' death and allowed my wife and I to travel the world with his Grace Baptist Church of Mount Vernon family.

The church building that Friendship purchased in 1998 is now a ministry that touches and services the community because Dr. Richardson challenged me to make it happen, and the Lord granted us favor. He is a hero in my life, and I am grateful for his love, wisdom, and encouragement.

I write this letter because young preachers need to know that success comes by signing up for mentorship and accountability. One can only become great by humbling himself and submitting to someone who will invest his life into yours.

Thank you, Doc. You have always had my back. My entire family loves you and your entire family.

Archbishop E. Bernard Jordan, founder of Zoe Ministries NYC

Witness to Grace: A Testimony of Favor is a book that, as you read it, you start to identify the abundance of God's grace that is made available to everyone who is willing to become a recipient and enter into this gift of grace. Richardson has discovered the power of grace throughout his life, and now he shares this grace with the readers and those who are willing to follow in this journey of grace. Grace is not fair. It gives you the winning edge, because it allows the hidden hand of God to open doors that were impossible to open. Reading the journey of Richardson allows you to be a witness to grace. As the saying goes, "A coincidence is a small miracle when God chooses to remain anonymous." Richardson documents the miracle moments of God, calling these miracles God's grace.

Dr. Dwight C. Jones, pastor, First Baptist Church, South Richmond, Virginia

Franklyn Richardson's *Witness to Grace: A Testimony of Favor* is a guide to Grace Consciousness and an understanding of the gracious guiding hand of God in the affairs of our lives. This book catalogs in intimate and personal detail the grace journey of one of the great preaching voices of our day. Dr. Richardson reminds us to recognize grace when it is evidenced in our lives. From a nineteen-year-old pastor to a saged successful leader of people and causes, Dr. Richardson's journey allows the reader to benefit from a life lived through the lens of grace.

Reverend Al Sharpton, founder and president, National Action Network, New York, New York

Dr. W. Franklyn Richardson embodies the qualities of 21st century seasoned social justice ministries unlike anyone else. Mentored by Dr. Sandy Ray (a close friend of Dr. Martin Luther King Jr.) and Dr. Wyatt Tee Walker (King's chief of staff), Richardson expanded Grace Baptist into one thriving Church in three locations, focused on ministry, empowerment, and equality. *Witness to Grace* is a testament to his remarkable journey. As chairman of the board of National Action Network, he has gone to jail and to the White House, while bearing the historic mantle of the Black Church's involvement in the pursuit of justice…

Dr. LaKeesha Walrond, president, New York Theological Seminary, New York, New York

Witness to Grace is a living testament to the power of grace in the midst of confusion, chaos, and calamity. As the Rev. Dr. W. Franklyn Richardson shares his deep and personal transformative encounters with God, he inspires us to hold fast to the strength of our ancestral heritage, overcoming through faith, words, and works. For Richardson, grace is not merely an abstract blessing to a faithful life but rather a tangible manifestation of God working in collaboration with humanity. The strength and determination expressed in his faith journey will encourage you to activate the power within your own spiritual journey.

Dr. Ralph Douglas West, pastor, The Church Without Walls, Houston, Texas

Much of theology is an autobiography, and if that is true, W. Franklyn Richardson is the embodiment of the theology of grace. So, it is not surprising that his memoir is titled *Witness to Grace: A Testimony of Favor.* As you read his life's story and meet his grandparents, his mother and father, his wife and children, his preaching uncles, and his Broadway entertaining brother and sister, Rich's entire journey is made up of a series of acts of grace and favor. Then it is not a coincidence that he would be called to pastor a church named Grace. In fact, it is divine providence.

Jim Winkler, general secretary and president, National Council of Churches

Rev. Dr. W. Franklyn Richardson is a giant in American Christianity and *Witness to Grace* makes clear why that is so. His deep faith, eloquence, indefatigability, curiosity, hopefulness, and passion are on full display in this beautiful and big-hearted memoir. He marries together in his life and ministry evangelism and social justice just as they should be, and he is forever fearless in working for it to be on earth as it is in heaven. I am grateful for his friendship and his commitment to the ecumenical cause.

Index

Abraham, 8, 34, 124
Adams, John Hurst, 176
African Council of Churches, 148
African Methodist Episcopal (AME), 173, 217
Alexander, Michelle, 201
Alfred Street Baptist Church, 118
Alpha Phi Omega, 26
April 1, 1975, 57
Austin, Samuel, 60, 129
Bailey, Pearl, 50
Banda, Hastings, 83
Baptist, 202
Baptist Convention USA, 80
Baptist Ministers Conference of Richmond and Vicinity, 42
Before the Parade Passes By, 50
Bensonhurst, 150
Bethany Baptist Church, 77, 118
Bethel Metropolitan Baptist Church, 135
Birmingham jail, 147
Black Church, 162, 163
Blackwood, Ronald A., 61, 62
Bluefield State University, 43
Bowers III, Frederick, 4
Bradford, John, 84
Bryant, John R., 217

About the Author

W. Franklyn Richardson is Senior Pastor of Grace Baptist Church in the City of Mount Vernon, New York, and Chairman of the Board at Virginia Union University, his alma mater. He also serves as chairman of the boards of the National Action Network and the Conference of National Black Churches. Richardson earned his divinity degree from Yale University Divinity School and his Doctor of Ministry as a Wyatt Tee Walker Fellow from the United Theological Seminary in Dayton, Ohio. Mentored by Dr. Sandy Ray (a close friend of Dr. Martin Luther King Jr.) and Dr. Wyatt Tee Walker (Dr. King's chief of staff), Richardson has received numerous honors and accolades. Two notable distinctions include induction into The Rev. Dr. Martin Luther King Jr. Board of Preachers and the International Hall of Honor by Morehouse College in Atlanta, Georgia and The Alumni Award for Distinction in Congregational Ministry from Yale University. Dr. Richardson is married to Inez Nunnally Richardson and lives in New York.